The Redemption of Black Elk

An Ancient Path to Inner Strength Following the Footprints of the Lakota Holy Man

by
Linda L. Stampoulos

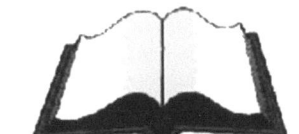

CCB Publishing
British Columbia, Canada

The Redemption of Black Elk: An Ancient Path to Inner
Strength Following the Footprints of the Lakota Holy Man

Copyright ©2010 by Linda L. Stampoulos
ISBN-13 978-1-926585-91-8
Second Edition

Library and Archives Canada Cataloguing in Publication
Stampoulos, Linda L., 1946-
The redemption of Black Elk : an ancient path to inner strength following the
footprints of the Lakota holy man / written by Linda L. Stampoulos – 2nd ed.
ISBN 978-1-926585-91-8
Also available in electronic format.
1. Black Elk, 1863-1950. 2. Oglala Indians--Religion. 3. Spiritual life.
I. Title.
E98.R3S75 2010   299.7   C2010-904661-7

For all general information regarding other books, visit pompanobooks.com

The cover: Pictured is Hehaka Sapa, Black Elk, a Holy Man of the Oglala Sioux. Photograph courtesy of the National Park Service, Little Bighorn Battlefield National Monument. Catalog number 17198.

Extreme care has been taken to ensure that all information presented in this book is accurate and up to date at the time of publishing. Neither the author nor the publisher can be held responsible for any errors or omissions. Additionally, neither is any liability assumed for damages resulting from the use of the information contained herein.

All rights reserved. No part of this publication may be reproduced, stored in a retrieval system or transmitted in any form or by any means, electronic, mechanical, photocopying, recording or otherwise without the express written permission of the publisher. Printed in the United States of America and the United Kingdom.

Publisher: CCB Publishing
             British Columbia, Canada
             www.ccbpublishing.com

Dedication

To look ahead and see what we may become, we must first look back to see how our past has enriched us. I dedicate this work to two men who lived during the same winters although several thousand miles apart. The first man is my Great-Grandfather Otto Wolf, a humble cobbler who lived in the village of Gommla in Thuringia, Germany. He dedicated his life to the care and comfort of sixteen children, the oldest of whom was my grandmother Ella. The second man is Black Elk, a Lakota holy man who shared this humility and dedicated his life to his family and his belief. The strength and conviction of these two men serve as markers of courage for me to look ahead and see what I may become.

Contents

Acknowledgments vi
Black Elk's Lament ix
Introduction xii
Find your Sacred Place 1
Draw your Sacred Hoop 15
Name your Heroes and your Demons 34
Find your Center 50
Nourish the Sacred Tree 66
Walk the Red Road 85
Epilogue: The Great Vision 94
Suggested Reading 133

Acknowledgments

First and foremost, I would like to thank the John G. Neihardt Trust for allowing me access to the body of work of Mr. Neihardt which was so vital for my research. I am also grateful for their permission to publish sections of the original transcriptions of Mr. Neihardt's 1931 Interviews with Black Elk on the Pine Ridge Reservation, and the set of stenographic notes and transcriptions completed by his daughters Enid and Hilda Neihardt.

Most special acknowledgment to the teachings of Mr. Joseph Campbell, whose lifetime of dedication to the study of mythology proved invaluable to this work. As one of the world's foremost authorities on mythology, Joseph Campbell devoted himself to bringing the mythical sense of the world and its eternal figures back into our everyday consciousness.

My sincere appreciation is given to John C. Knozal, Manuscript Specialist, of the Western Historical Manuscript Collection, University of Missouri-Columbia, Columbia, Missouri for promptly sending me the rolls of microfilm from the John G. Neihardt Special Collection necessary for my research.

My thanks is given to Coi Drummond-Gehrig, Photo Consultant, Western History's Collection, Denver Public Library for her prompt and excellent service.

Thanks to the National Park Service, Little Bighorn Battlefield National Monument for providing the cover photograph of Black Elk.

Special thanks to Kenneth Shields Jr., a Dakota Sioux from the Bad Temper Bear Band, currently living on the Fort Peck Indian Reservation. He spent several years as Director of the Tribal Archives, and is a contributing author for the tribal newspaper, Wotanin Wowapi. Kenny has been a long-time friend and in addition to his assistance with cultural interpretations, has always offered needed encouragement.

I also express my appreciation to Donovin A. Sprague, an accomplished author, historian, and descendant of Chief Hump and family descendant of Chief Crazy Horse, for his assistance with the Lakota translations. Donovin is also an enrolled tribal member of the Cheyenne River Sioux., the Director of Education at the Crazy Horse Memorial, an instructor at Black Hills State University, Oglala Lakota College, and the Indian University of North America at Crazy Horse Memorial.

Special thanks to Jack Aquila and his staff at Inter-City Press for their imagination and creativity in assisting with the illustrations in this book.

My thanks to John Lamaestra and his staff at Arch-Angel Productions for all the wonderful work in developing and maintaining our website *pompanobooks.com*.

I would like to thank my husband Scott for his review and word processing assistance. Thanks too, to my son Evan and my daughter-in-law Cathy for their technical contributions to this work.

Thanks and acknowledgement to Cinnamon Bear Alwin, a caring Lenape woman who served as my primary reader and cultural reference.

Recognition goes to Bruce and Lucy Baker, and Herbert and Sylvia Benz for serving as my footprints to my German translator, Rainer Hoeh who shares the understanding and importance of this work. Thanks too for Sylvia and Herbert's willingness to serve as readers for the German translation.

To my family, the Aschoffs, Schaefers, and Reinharts, as well as my friends who offered patience, understanding, and words of encouragement during the three years of this project I thank you all.

The Meditative Readings and the Great Vision narrative are excerpts from "The 1931 Interviews by John G. Neihardt" published with the permission of the John G. Neihardt Trust and the Western Historical Manuscript Collection, University of Missouri-Columbia, Columbia, MO.

All photographs were provided with the permission of the Western History's Collection, Denver Public Library.

Black Elk's Lament
(1931, age 67)

I am going to tell you the story of my life and if it were only the story of my life I think I would not tell it, for what is one man that he should make much of his winters even when they bend him like a heavy snow?

But now that I see it all as from a lonely hilltop, I know it was the story of a mighty vision given in my youth to a man too weak to use it; of a holy tree that should have flourished in a people's heart with flowers and singing birds, and now is withered; and of a people's dream that died in the bloody snow. It was a beautiful dream.

But if the vision was true and mighty, as I know it is true and mighty yet; for such things are of the spirit, and it is in the darkness of their eyes that men get lost.

You see me now a pitiful old man who has done nothing; for the nation's hoop is broken and scattered. There is no center any longer, and the sacred tree is dead.

O Great Spirit, I recall the great vision you sent me. It may be that some little root of the sacred tree still lives. Nourish it then, that it may leaf and bloom and fill with singing birds. Hear me not for myself, but for my people; I am old. Hear me that they may once more go back into the sacred hoop and find the good red road, and the shielding tree. O make my people live!

Excerpts from "Black Elk Speaks by John G. Neihardt" with permission of the John G. Neihardt Trust and the Western Historical Manuscript Collection, University of Missouri-Columbia, Columbia, MO.

This outdoor photograph of Black Elk was taken in 1936 by Joseph G. Masters. Photo is provided courtesy of the Denver Public Library, Western History Collection, Call Number X33351.

Introduction

Most texts devoted to self-help and self-exploration concern themselves with providing tools and exercises for individual application to today's problems. The approach taken in this book is to lift you up and carry you back to a time when America was experiencing perhaps the greatest upheaval of its indigenous populations and their culture. Provided are Meditative Readings that serve as your window to the past; eyewitness accounts of benchmark events in the history of the West.

But this is much more than an historical recording. By exploring the first hand accounts, the author discovered an ancient pathway woven into the images of that time. What surfaced was a series of metaphorical footprints left behind by a man named Black Elk.

As a young child of the Oglala Lakota Sioux, Black Elk had been given a vision; a mighty vision which would lead him on a personal journey intended to result in the peace and flourishing of his people. He was born in December of 1863, the year tribes recorded as, "The Winter when the Four Crows Were Killed." Far to the east America was engaged in the great Civil War. Very little attention was given to happenings in the West.

During his early childhood, Black Elk and the people of the Sioux Nation were free to live their lives as they had for centuries. As a boy he learned to fish, to hunt and use a bow, to ride, and to take part in the celebrations so vital to the life of the tribe. A simple man, Black Elk never learned to read or write, he spoke only Lakota, yet amazingly this one simple man would live to experience more cultural upheaval in his early years than most of us would experience in a lifetime.

Over the course of his life, Black Elk would find himself at the Battle of the Little Big Horn; at Fort Robinson when his cousin, the great leader Crazy Horse, was killed; in exile with Sitting Bull and Gall; and at Wounded Knee during the time of the Ghost Dance movement and the Great Massacre. He was witness to the government's unrelenting efforts to take from the Lakota their sacred Black Hills, and even beyond the land, their very way of life.

With the help of his mighty vision, Black Elk was able to unfold symbols and metaphors in very unique ways so that the lessons learned built on one another and, in the end, laid out before us an ancient path toward inner strength and a balanced life. Black Elk's symbols and metaphors present themselves in guises or clothes that often must be peeled back or carefully removed to discover the messages they contain. There is nothing new here; basic truths that exist throughout time. The challenge is to lift those meanings from one generation into another so that in re-examining them we too may have the direction, a way for us to go.

Black Elk's life was truly a journey. It began some one hundred and twenty five years ago, it had about it a sacredness that must never be forgotten, because for him it was never forgotten. Now, however, as an old man of many winters, he pours forth a soulful lament of one who has done "nothing." The once beautiful dream died in the bloody snow and without the fulfillment of the vision, his people will continue to be lost in the "darkness of their eyes."

Great men, however, are never as far away from hope as they may think. So it is that up from the depths of his broken heart he once more pleads to *Wakan Tanka*, "If it may be that some little root of the sacred tree still lives, nourish it then that it may leaf and bloom and fill with singing birds." Black Elk died believing the dream was lost. But this is far from the truth.

It was impossible for him to see how with each step of his personal journey he left a footprint for us to follow. Step by step the way has been made for each of us.

Why then, would this man who lived over a century ago need redemption? The answer is as simple as the life he lived: The rediscovery of a dream. Black Elk's vision was a prophetic message telling the terrible future of his tribe. But his vision also held positive aspects that must be reclaimed. It is through this reclamation that the guiding beacons given to him will cause the ancient path to rise up out of the bloody snow and show the way for us…125 years later. He thought the message of the vision would die with him, but it can be brought to life again through us.

The journey we travel in life is certainly not new. History tells us of those who traveled before, each with their own set of problems. But history can also tell us <u>how</u> people throughout the centuries found ways to cope with their problems. That message can be as important, if not more important than the history lesson itself.

Why not, then, examine someone else's journey and discover the ancient path they took? Someone like Black Elk, who experienced enormous problems: harsh winters, lack of food, battles with neighboring tribes, the encroachment of White soldiers who were intent to strip away his entire way of life. Yet he found a pathway to overcome them; and by doing so, reaches across a century of time and points the way for us. Our problems are in no way similar. For most of us, the problems concern themselves with interpersonal relationships, lack of money, employment, and health. It is in this highly technological world, that we become increasingly separated from the ability to see a path and lead a balanced life.

The messages of his vision challenged Black Elk with the raw material; but for him they became as a Rubik's cube in his hands which no matter how he twisted and turned it, the squares never clicked into balance. The Rubik's cube is an attractive, compelling object in which the goal appears deceptively simple: twist the levels of the cube until all the colored squares line up in harmony. Most people give up early on. Others, however keep turning and twisting seeking the mysterious clicks that lead to completion.

To help with an interpretation of Black Elk's account, the author invoked the insight of Joseph Campbell, one of the world's foremost authorities on mythology: the stories and legends told by human beings through the ages to explain the universe and their place in it. He devoted himself to bringing the mythical sense of the world and its eternal figures back into our everyday consciousness. Campbell credits such German scholars as Heinrich Zimmer, and Arthur Schopenhauer, as well as Swiss psychiatrist Carl Jung, who influenced his interpretations during his career.

Joseph Campbell was very familiar with the story of Black Elk, and noted his special gift of insight. Generations after the time of Black Elk, Joseph Campbell found himself working the same metaphors and symbols. The "cube" was now in his hands so to speak and, remarkably, in the twisting and turning of the cube he emerged with curiously similar truths pointing us to the same ancient path. Through his insights of symbol and metaphor Campbell was able to examine the metaphorical footprints and provide us with a twenty-first century "spin" that a simple man generations before could only imagine.

Black Elk left a legacy not only to his own people, but to anyone who is willing to pick up the symbols and metaphors and follow the ancient path. In his dream and great vision as well as his life journey he left the lessons to attain peace and wholeness within oneself as well as within an entire society.

Now the "cube" is in our hands and since our lives are

often more off-balance than not, we know even without looking that the cube is "all mixed up." This book offers a new look at Black Elk's footprints and together with the insight of Joseph Campbell, presents a path with the twists and turns to help click our lives into balance.

As we walk in Black Elk's footprints, it is important that we come to know more about him and his life. Throughout the journey, there are Meditative Readings, his actual words from the 1931 Interviews with John Neihardt, that provide insight into events of his life and his reflections regarding them. The Talking Points that follow, connect the event of his life journey with the metaphorical footprint.

We begin with the first step...

The Journey begins...

Oyanke

Wakan

Find your Sacred Place...

Find your Sacred Place

To live a full life one must appreciate the mysterious forces that not only surround us but run through us. Call it what you will: spirit, energy, power, consciousness, Chi, the idea is the same: this "life force" is in every living thing, animal and plant. One key to a full and balanced life is understanding how to manage and maximize this force. A person need not recognize the FULL nature of such a life source, indeed many people live their entire lives on a "hit and miss" approach, not really knowing or grasping its full potential.

To connect to such a force it would seem of primary importance that a person consciously put himself in a setting conducive to apprehending the experience.

Joseph Campbell felt it was absolutely necessary that a person make time and take time to be completely alone, separated from the daily grind of endless demands, and enter a sacred place. A *sacred place*, according to Joseph Campbell, is an absolute necessity for anybody today. He uses this term to describe a special place, a certain time of day that you can visit to remove yourself from the world around you. When you are there, you don't know what's in the newspapers, you don't concern yourself with your finances or the other thoughts that can invade your peacefulness. This is a place of creative incubation, he states, a place where you can experience and bring forth what you are or what you might be.

It can be as simple as listening to your favorite music, reading the book you've always wanted, or even closing your eyes and shutting out the noise of the world. At first nothing happens, but he assures us, if you have a sacred place and learn to use it, something will happen. You will begin to get the "thou" feeling of life.

The first step on our journey of inner exploration is to provide ourselves with a setting, an actual location from which we can begin. If we follow Black Elk's footprints, we will see that he often would travel out into the Plains, alone, to think and be at one with himself. His whole world was free and peaceful, with little or no distractions. How different from our world.

Set the alarm, get ready for work, do the shopping, balance the check book, the demands of our lives go on and on. There is ALWAYS something required of us to do. More often we get so involved in our everyday activities that we hardly know where we are. The claims of the environment can be so great, most of our actions are economically or socially determined and so very demanding. These things do not come out of our life, they penetrate into it.

Selection of one's sacred place varies from person to person. In general it's best if it is outdoors, close to a natural setting. Nature provides subliminal triggers, ancient triggers, firing energy into memory cells gone dormant. These "sparks" will ignite a nostalgic mood, familiar yet unfamiliar, imprinted wiring that will lend itself to deeper thought or insight.

The individual begins his meditation with a certain state of mind, a level of awareness which will eventually lead itself to its own "energy" source. Joseph Campbell referred to this as a level of consciousness, something beyond awareness. It is a connection to a greater consciousness beyond that of one's own and shared by all. It will be as strong and as deep as you allow yourself to move into it. Everyone has the capacity to move from their everyday happenings into this other place, a place where your mind and body want to go. No one can tell you where your serenity is, everyone must learn to recognize it on their own. But when you even have a small recognition of where it lies, "grab it" says Campbell, and you will put yourself on a track that has been there waiting for you all the time.

Meditation can serve the same function. It places individual awareness on a higher platform allowing one to "listen to the body's own spirituality and heart life." This life song is inside each of us. "The world is full of people," Campbell goes on, "who have stopped listening to themselves." They go with society's demands and live a life that their inner voice is not interested in at all.

And so the journey along the ancient path begins: finding a sacred place and igniting the first beacon. The following Meditative Reading introduces Black Elk as he talks about the experiences of his early years living in his "sacred place" on the Great Plains.

Meditative Reading

The Thunder-Beings Speak
A Message of Fire and Ice

Black Elk recalls his life as a young boy. He tells of his early visions, the voices calling to him, and at age nine, receiving the Great Vision.

My name is Black Elk, I am 67 years old. I was born on Little Powder River in 1863, the Winter When the Four Crows Were Killed on the Tongue River. To begin with, I am the fourth of the name Black Elk. My father was a medicine man and was brother to several other medicine men. My father was cousin to Crazy Horse's father.

When I was four years old, I played a little here and there and while playing I would hear a voice singing now and then, but I did not catch it very well then. The first time I rode a horse I was five years old and my father made me some bows and arrows. This was in the spring. I was out in the woods trying to get a bird and just as I was going into the woods there was a thunderstorm coming and I heard a voice over there. This was not a dream, it actually happened. I saw two men coming out of a cloud with spears. As I was looking up to that, there was a kingbird sitting there and these two men were coming toward me singing the sacred song and that bird told me to listen to the two men. The kingbird said: "Look, the clouds all over are one-sided, a voice is calling to you. I looked up and the two men were coming down singing:

> Behold him, a sacred voice is calling you.
> All over the sky a sacred voice is calling you

I stood gazing at them and they were coming from the north; then they started toward the west and were geese. This vision lasted about twenty minutes.

When I was six years old, it seemed that at times I would hear something calling me, and then at other times I would forget entirely about this voice.

It was 1873, I was now almost ten years old. Close to the Crow Camp on the Little Big Horn I was riding along and I heard something calling me again. Just before we got to Greasy Grass Creek (the Little Big Horn), they camped again for the night. There was a man by the name of Man Hip who invited me for supper. While eating I heard a voice. I heard someone say, "It is time, now they are calling you." I knew then that I was called upon by the spirits so I thought I'd just go where they wanted me to. As I came out of the tent both of my thighs hurt me.

The next morning they broke camp and I started out with some others on horseback. We stopped at a creek to get a drink. When I got off my horse I crumbled down and I couldn't walk. The boys helped me up and when the people camped again, I was very sick. They went on, taking me to the Sioux band camp and I was still pretty sick. Both my legs and arms were swollen badly and even my face. This all came suddenly.

As I lay in the tipi I could see through the tipi the same two men whom I saw before and they were coming from the clouds, Then I recognized them as the same men I had seen before my first vision. They came and stood off aways from me and stopped, saying: "Hurry up, your grandfather is calling you." When they started back I got up and started to follow them. Just as I got out of the tipi I could see the two men going back into the clouds and there was a small cloud coming down toward me at the same time, which stood before me. I got on top of the cloud and was raised up, following the two men, and when I looked back, I saw my father and mother looking at me. When I looked back I felt sorry that I was leaving them.

Black Elk Is Given the Great Vision
(included in its entirety as a conclusion to this narrative)

The next thing I heard was somebody saying: "The boy is feeling better now, you had better give him some water." I looked up and saw it was my mother and father stooping over me. They were giving me some medicine but it was not that that cured me—it was my vision that cured me. The first thought that came to me was that I had been traveling and my father and mother didn't seem to know that I had been gone and they didn't look glad. I felt very sad over this.

I felt that my mother and father did not welcome me and when I came to, I found out that my whole body was swollen and puffed. As I thought about it, I knew that I had gone someplace. Standing Bear's uncle was a medicine man called Whirlwind Chaser and he was treating me at this time. When I came to I felt better and wanted to go out and run around right away, but my parents wouldn't let me. Next morning I was myself again and the vision was, of course, still in my mind. When they broke camp I thought it over and thought it was a wonderful place I went to. I thought the people should know it and I felt as though I wanted them to know about it. I pondered over it and at times I did not want to think about it. The medicine man got a great name because I was cured by him.

The next day we reached the Soldiers' Camp. There were only about twenty tipis of the Oglalas that were traveling to the fort—the main band stayed back. When we reached the camp we scattered out among the relatives of ours. I had an aunt there and I made camp there right beside her tipi. Part of the Oglalas camped by the White Butte at Fort Robinson.

We stayed all winter at Fort Robinson. I was now ten years old. The only thing we did here was to make Indian sleds and coast down the hills and we also whipped the tops on the ice. The sleds were made out of jaws and ribs of buffalo, tied together with rawhide.

During the Spring we started back to the Tongue River and camped at Fort Keogh. We had a sun dance here. After the sun dance I recalled my vision and I was very much in fear and it seemed as though I hated to see a cloud. I could hear the Thunder-beings calling. I could understand the birds whenever they sang. When a cloud appeared with the birds it seemed that they would say: "Behold your grandfathers; make haste." From here on I couldn't get along with men – I had to get out and think about this and I knew all the time I had something to do but I couldn't figure out what it was that I was to do that I didn't do. I was always afraid of the spirits. All this summer I thought that every time there was lightning and thunderstorms I was afraid. I just pondered and wondered and thought and it seemed that I just held back, but I did not want to tell my mother and father, for they would think I was getting odd again. I would take my horse and go out by myself and compare everything on earth with the things in my vision. I was glad that it was getting fall because the Thunder-beings would quit coming, because I feared the Thunder-beings so bad.

In the moon when the ponies shed (May) we broke camp again and we started for the Black Hills to cut tipi poles for the tipis. There were about thirty tipis in the band now.

As I looked up I heard the shrill whistle of an eagle and I wondered if this eagle wasn't the one of my vision, which was guarding me. I thought also that the people around me might be the nation of my vision. Whenever I saw a cloud appearing it seemed that someone was coming to see me and that some day it would be a duty for me to do something for my nation.

Next morning men got on horses and got axes ready to get tipi poles, They followed the Rapid Creek into the hills and into the thick of the forest and began cutting tipi poles, There were lots of slim poles, for no one at this time had bothered them at all. They brought them back and began to strip and dress the poles. Some of us knew how to strip them and some did not, so the work was rather slow. Men had gone out on a hunt so we had plenty of meat—bear meat, etc. We were sitting around camp boiling bear meat. Next morning we were all through with the poles and we began building a sweat tipi for a medicine man by the name of Chips. He was the first man who made a sacred ornament for Crazy Horse to use in the war and probably this is where Crazy Horse was made bullet-proof and got his bullet-proof power.

When we got back to the people at Fort Robinson we told them that we saw some whites going toward the Black Hills. It was heard that the soldiers were up there to get the white and yellow metals in the hills. Everyone thought that something should be done about it and they must get together and decide on something. They called the Indians who stayed around the fort "Sticks around the Fort," and the thought of them as sticking up for the whites. Crazy Horse was on the west and Sitting Bull was on the north and everyone thought they should get together and do something about the gold-diggers in the Black Hills. Red Cloud's people said that the soldiers had come up there to drive the gold-diggers out, but the northern Indians did not believe it.

They had a sun dance here at Fort Robinson for the people's health and for an abundance of meat. Some of them were dancing before they were going to war. I remember that only two men danced this sun dance because one of them was dancing on one leg and had lost one in the battle of the

Hundred Slain. The other man had two good legs but he had lost one eye in the same battle. So the two men danced with three eyes and three legs.

We youngsters went down to the creek while they were sun dancing and we got some elm leaves and put them in a sack and we would fill our mouths with slippery elm leaves and we'd slash this stuff on the people when they were trying to look their best in the sun dance. We even would do this to some of the older people. Everyone was supposed to be teasing each other and everyone was happy that day. This was a kind of an endurance. Men should stand lots of endurance in the sun dance and we boys were there to test the endurance of their minds.

At the sun dances the children are taken, and the medicine men pierce their ears and if the parents think a lot of their children, they must give away a pony for each piercing. These ponies were given to the poor. Or a person who has performed a brave deed has the right to pierce a child's ear the same as a medicine man has.

In the fall we broke camp and started toward the Little Big Horn. While we were at Fort Robinson we could see immigrants coming up to the Black Hills for gold and this was in the year of the treaty of 1876. I was there at the time of the powwow for the arrangement of the treaty of 1875. All I could remember is that in the middle of the circle of the tipis they put up a shade of canvas and underneath this were the white and Indian councilors and all around them were Indians on horseback. This was on the north side of White River, at the mouth of White Clay Creek. I was only a boy then, so this was all I saw of the making of the treaty. I wondered about the treaty so I asked my father what it was. He told me that the soldiers had wanted to lease the Black Hills. The general said to the Indians that if they did not lease the Black Hills to the

Grandfather at Washington, the Black Hills would be just like snow held in the hand and melting away. In other words, they were going to take the Black Hills (Kha Sapa) away from us anyway.

Linda L. Stampoulos

Talking Points:

The Thunder-Beings Speak

Imagine a hot, clear summer day on the Great Plains. Without warning, the sky suddenly darkens, flashes of light strike the tops of the cottonwood trees, setting them ablaze. At the same time sheets of hail, the size of golf balls batter the ground. Fire and ice from the same angry storm. To the Sioux Indians these were Spirit forms, hard to understand yet very powerful. They were *wakan.* These Thunder-beings who controlled the fire and the ice had both the power to kill and the power to heal. According to Black Elk, from this water all healing herbs grow.

When people of the twenty-first century experience violent storms, one of their first concerns is the interruption of power and the many inconveniences of having to do without electricity for a time. The wonder and magnificence of nature is often lost to the complaint of a "missed" television program or a scramble for candles so often misplaced after the last storm.

The Indians of the Plains, however, lived in a world of nature and experienced its tremendous power all the time. Campbell notes, "just being there, you feel the wonder and you become aware of something larger than the human personification of the energies that exist."

Black Elk's experience was not one of peace and soliloquy. As a youth he lived in fear of the Thunder-beings. Continually he would leave his sacred space with a restlessness and passion and return to his people to fulfill the many charges presented him. He would hear the Thunder-beings calling him, but did not know what they wanted. His family watched him hide whenever the storms came, leading them to believe that he had dreamed of thunder.

In Lakota belief, a person who dreams of thunder must perform a ceremony acting out his *heyoka* dream. The dreamer must obey the command of the Thunder-beings. As part of the obligation, the *heyoka* ceremony has the dreamer deliberately act like a clown and do things backwards to make people laugh.

The medicine men of his village encouraged Black Elk to enact the horse dance rather than a *heyoka* ceremony. This performance demonstrated the first part of his great vision. It was after the horse dance that Black Elk said "After this ceremony was completed, it seemed that I was happy to see my people and they looked renewed and happy. I was now recognized as a medicine man at age seventeen. Everyone had respect for me. The fear that I had had now all disappeared and when the Thunder-beings came I was always glad to see them come, as they came as relatives.

The security of a sacred place can be comforting. It serves as a warm retreat from the often harsh realities of our world. It is important to remember, though, that one MUST venture out into the world again as Black Elk did, to meet today's challenges. One could think of it as temporary oasis, giving us the opportunity for reflection and renewal as we make our life journey.

Throughout his interviews with John Neihardt, Black Elk would reference the symbols and metaphors given to him in his vision, some more powerful than others. We continue our journey with perhaps the most powerful and most referenced in all his teachings, the Sacred Hoop.

This teenage girl seems to have found her sacred place on the bank of the Little Bighorn River. Entitled "The voice of the Water Spirits" photographer Joseph K. Dixon captured a tranquil and reflective moment of her day. The photo is dated between 1908 and 1913 and is provided by the Denver Public Library, Western History Collection, Call Number Z3182.

Can'glegska Wakan

Draw your Sacred Hoop

Linda L. Stampoulos

Draw your Sacred Hoop

After you have selected your sacred place and become familiar with the peaceful reflection and solitude it affords, you are ready to follow the next footprint left by Black Elk. You are now asked to *Draw Your Sacred Hoop.* Keep in mind that each of the symbolic metaphors given to Black Elk in his vision is open to various interpretations and that of the Sacred Hoop is no exception. One might say there are several interpretations of his vision hoop. There is the Sacred Hoop of Containment and Protection which will be discussed in this section; the Sacred Hoop of Harmony which is highlighted in the Talking Points of the Little Bighorn account; and finally, the Sacred Hoop as the Circle of Winters detailed in the next chapter. Before exploring each of these interpretations, consider the following words of Black Elk, telling of the Sacred Hoop presented to him in the great vision:

The Sacred Hoop

> Four more riders, one from each quarter, came forth and presented me with a hoop, and with that hoop I was to make a nation and under that we were to prosper. The circle represented the old people that represented a nation. The center of it represented the prosperity of the nation. I was to raise a nation either in prosperity or

in difficulty. In presenting the sacred hoop to me, the spirit from the west said: "Behold this sacred hoop; it is the people you shall have." You realize that in the sacred hoop we will multiply. You will notice that everything the Indian does is in a circle. Everything that they do is the power from the sacred hoop, but you see today that this house is not in a circle. It is a square. It is not the way we should live. The Great Spirit assigned us a certain religion and etc. The power won't work in anything but circles. Everything is now too square. The sacred hoop is vanishing among the people. We get even tents that are square and live in them. Even the birds and their nests are round. You take the bird's eggs and put them in a square nest and the mother bird just won't stay there. We Indians are relative-like to the birds. Everything tries to be round—the world is round. We Indians have been put here to be like the wilds and we cooperate with them. Their eggs of generations are in the sacred hoop to hatch out. Now the white man has taken away our nest and put us in a box and here they ask us to hatch our children, but we cannot do it. We are vanishing in this box.

In his great vision, Black Elk saw the eventual breaking of his people's hoop, and in his lament he tells its painful meaning. The story does not end here. The rediscovery of his dream would have us mend the hoop, starting with our own personal circle.

The Sacred Hoop of Containment and Protection

Joseph Campbell tells us, the circle can be thought as the psychological expression of the totality of one's self. Simply stated, circles shut out the outside and hold in the inside.

When you are in your sacred place, the next step is to draw an imaginary circle that contains only those elements of your life that are of most concern to you and which are at least to some degree, under your control. This exercise accomplishes two things: first it delimits the issues you need to address and are most on your mind; and second, it blocks out those more distant issues that are beyond your control. For our personal journey, the concept of the circle is one in which you are asked to define the limits of your immediate concerns, both positive and negative.

Your sacred hoop then, is in effect you. It gives you a oneness, a whole being. The focus now becomes inward. The hoop's containment gives you a feeling of control. By definition we are now able to see exactly what you must face. The issues shrink to fit inside and become more manageable and less overwhelming. It is through these concepts of "shrinkage" and "containment" that the elements of your life are reduced to their proper proportions.

This is no easy task. In the beginning your hoop will contain many issues beyond your control. Throughout the day we face issues ranging from our local arena to world events well beyond our locus of control. It is our nature to take on the problems of the world in an effort to do good. Drawing the hoop of containment does not mean that broader issues will be ignored. On the contrary, the exercise is meant to build a good base where one can construct inner strength and have a solid place to move out into the world again.

Joseph Campbell often referred to the power symbolized by the circle. It represents a totality, he explained, a unit with no beginning and no end. It is an ever-present thing, the center from which you have come and back to where you go. He quotes Carl Jung's description, "the circle is the most powerful religious symbol, it is one of the great primeval images of mankind; in considering the circle, you are analyzing yourself."

Jung believed that the totality or the content of your circle comprises all the issues you are aware of (consciousness), and a personal unconsciousness which he defines as chiefly those issues which at one time have been conscious but which have disappeared from consciousness through having been forgotten or repressed. It is the combination of the conscious and the personal unconscious that Jung refers to as "the self" and claims both exist within the circle you have drawn.

We continue our journey of exploration by looking inward, secure in the knowledge that we have the peace and protection of our sacred hoop. Black Elk and his people enjoyed this harmony in their last days of freedom on the Great Plains.

Linda L. Stampoulos

Meditative Reading

The Tiospaye at the Little Bighorn
The Final Days of the Sacred Hoop

Black Elk gives the account leading up to the Tiospaye gathering and the Battle with Custer's 7th Calvary at the Little Bighorn.

We broke camp and went to join Crazy Horse's band on the Tongue River. Then I went up into the Black Hills alone and had another vision under a tree and found out that the duty that was to come to me was that I would probably save the Black Hills. It looked as though it was impossible, but I was anxious to perform my duty on earth.

I was anxious to see my cousin Crazy Horse but he wasn't there. He must have been on a warpath against the Crows.

<u>Black Elk Tells About the Custer Battle</u>

It was late in the Spring of 1876 when we went to join the others camped at the Little Bighorn. We took our horses out on the prairie beyond to graze them. We had about ten thousand ponies—so many you couldn't count them. So many tipis we couldn't count them also. We were guarding our horses. The women were out hunting turnips and the men were out hunting also. We had guards all around. The boys and the old men were taking a bath in the Little Bighorn River, which was flowing pretty full from the June rise. I was so young yet and I wasn't very dependable, but in a case like this some of the boys asked me to go swimming.

I knew then that something terrible was going to happen

within a day. I thought about the bow and arrows the spirits had given me. I thought lots of things in a short time there that couldn't be imagined.

At daybreak my father woke me up and told me to go with him to take the horses out to graze. A cousin of mine and I were getting ready to take several horses out to graze. Then as I started, my father told me to be careful and I ought to have one horse with a long rope on it, easy to catch, and we should keep our eyes on the camp and look around us always. He said, "If anything happens bring horses back to camp right away as soon as you can." We took the horses out and herded them as the sun was coming out. We stood out there until the sun came up higher. We just let the horses go and I tied a long rope to one of them and turned them all loose. We went back to the camp. It was getting warm now and so the people were all swimming in the river. Some men went out hunting and women were out digging turnips and it was about eight or nine o'clock. We had no breakfast and had to go back to get it. Everyone took his horses to water.

I did not feel right—I had a funny feeling all this time, because I thought that in an hour or so something terrible might happen. The boys were all swimming and I did not go down because I did not feel very good. I made up my mind I would go swimming anyway, so I greased up my body. At the Hunkpapas I heard the crier saying: "They are charging, the chargers are coming. Where the tipi is they say the chargers are coming. (The tipi where they had put their dead before when they came down to the Greasy Grass.) Then the crier at the Oglalas announced it and then each village announced it one after the other. We heard the cry going from village to village.

Just about this time my cousin had taken the horses to water and they were then just coming from the water. I had a buckskin mare and got her. Everyone was catching their horses at this time. We were lucky to get our horses—most of the people's horses were out grazing yet they were running after them.

My brother came up and took hold of his horse and told me to go on back, but I had a six-shooter with me, which my sister had given me; and I had given my brother his gun. There were woods on the other side of the Hunkpapas. All the men got together and gathered in front of the woods. My brother hit for the bush. He told me to turn back, but I took after him. When I got to the timber the soldiers were shooting above us and you could see the leaves falling down off the trees where the bullets struck. I went in there and after that I did not know what happened back of me. We got under the brush little by little and we crossed the flat and the soldiers began to shoot at us and all we heard was: "Take courage, don't be like a woman." Some of them said, "Take courage, the helpless are out of their breath."

The women were running to the hills. Little bunches at a time began to cross the flat. I was underneath in the brush and I did not quite notice what happened above me. I stood there under the trees and recalled my vision there again and it made me feel stronger. Then I thought that my people in my vision had been Thunder-beings, but I didn't see why the soldiers should be doing this. I thought then that perhaps the people had used some of my power because I knew that we were going to wipe out the soldiers.

Close after the crying about courage we heard that Crazy Horse was coming. He was riding a white-faced horse. Everyone hollered: "Crazy Horse is coming!" Just then I heard the bunch on the hillside to the west crying: "Hokahey!" and making the tremolo. We heard also the eagle bone whistles. I knew from this shouting that the Indians were coming for I could hear the thunder of the ponies charging. A little above us

I could hear the hoofs of the soldiers' horses that went down into the brush. Then after a little while, they [the soldiers] went back up again and I followed after them. It was a bad mixture then—soldiers, then Indians, etc. I could see nothing much but I heard shots and voices. We all hollered at each other: "Hurry, Hurry!"

The soldiers were running by this time up the stream—soldiers and Indians mixed up. Just then I could see a Sioux charge at one of the soldiers and try to get a hold of his horse and the soldier shot the Sioux off his horse with the revolver he had. Then I saw that this white man had shot two of the Indians at this time. Before we knew it, the soldiers were firing on us and the women and children were fleeing for their lives.

While on top of the hill with my mother I could see the battle going on across the Little Bighorn. We could not see much because of the dust and the buzzing of the bullets and shots. At the same time the women were singing and sending tremolos out. At about this time about six boys asked me to go with them and we started down on ponies. Up a little further there was a ravine and we crossed through this. As we went down the hill we could see the gray horses coming toward the water on their stampede. Then we crossed the Little Bighorn and were nearly up and we could hear them hollering more and we could see the soldiers coming down the hill. They were making their arms go as though they were running, but they were only walking. We could see some Indians right on top of them whirling around all over the place. It seems as though the Indians could have just trampled them down even if we had not had weapons. Before we got there, the whites were all wiped out.

The women were here at this time. We went up on top and saw gray horses lying around where Custer was on top of the hill. You could see only a few Indians here by that time because most of the Indians' bodies had been taken away before this.

About this time the Indians began to gather the dead. There were two Sioux who got killed and their relatives came and got them and wrapped them in a blanket to take back. Then I got tired of looking around here. I could still smell nothing but blood and gunpowder, so I got sick of it pretty soon. I was a very happy boy. I wasn't a bit sorry. I knew beforehand that this was going to happen. When Reno charged I thought about the people as my nation and that they were relative-like to Thunder and that the soldiers were very foolish to do this, so I knew they were going to get wiped out. On top the hill we gathered just the way we were and from here we went after our tipis. That night nobody slept—everyone was up.

They were signaling from the camp with looking glasses when the sun was getting low in the afternoon, to the warriors. My mother was riding a mare with a colt and she tied it so that it would run right beside its mother and they would shoot at us while we were crossing this stream, but they did not hit us. Mother and I started back on the gallop to the camp. When we got back it was nearly sundown and at the same time there was another war party that came in from somewhere. They reported that there were soldiers coming upstream so we began to break camp.

Talking Points

The Tiospaye at the Little Bighorn
The Final Days of the Sacred Hoop

In June of 1876, a few days before America would mark its Centennial Celebration, a gathering of Indian people made history in a rich valley on the Little Bighorn River. Their legacy consists not of a victory in battle, but in the events that happened in the weeks prior to the arrival of Custer and his troops.

The Sacred Hoop of Harmony

It was Spring, in the Moon When the Ponies Shed, a time to celebrate new life and freedom, to follow the buffalo and other game. Men, women and children came to thank the Creator, *Wakan Tanka*, for safely bringing them through the harsh winter. They camped in the place where from ages past, they called the "Greasy Grass," a place of solitude and worship. There were a few lodges at first, but over a period of weeks, the gathering, often referred to as *Tiospaye* , or the Golden Encampment, would grow to become the largest in recorded American history. Eyewitnesses reported there being over 1,000 lodges, each leader with his own camp circle, with up to 7,000 people, almost 1,500 of them warriors. Among the many tribes represented, were the Yanktonais, Cheyenne, Arapaho, Dakota, and of the Lakota Sioux: the Oglala, Hunkpapa, Sicangu, Minnicoujou, Itazipco, Siha Sapa, and Oohenumpa. It is said that their tipi circles went from south to north.

Tatanka Iyotanka, Sitting Bull of the Hunkpapa, served as

the people's spiritual leader. Earlier that month, he had ordered a Sun Dance to be held in the nearby hills. The Sun Dance would purify the people and give them endurance. It was here that he had his vision of dead soldiers and horses falling into the Indian camp. Sitting Bull was a warrior and a visionary. He dedicated his life to preserve the beautiful culture of his people.

There was a powerful majesty surrounding the people in attendance, strong leaders who protected the tribes: Crazy Horse, Gall, American Horse, He Dog and their camp circles were joined as one statement of freedom. Black Elk was 13 years old at that time. It was four years earlier that, by a strange coincidence, his family was camped at this very site and he received his great vision.

During the day Black Elk recounts, the elders would sit in Counsel, women would dig turnips and prepare meals, the children swam in the river and rode their ponies. After dark, the drums would echo the heartbeat of the dancers and tales would be told victories and of the old ways. As Black Elk explained to Joseph Epes Brown,

> I should tell you why the drum is important to us. It is because the round form of the drum represents the whole universe, and its steady strong beat is the pulse, the heart, throbbing at the center of the universe. It is the voice of *Wakan Tanka*, and this sound stirs us and helps us to understand the mystery and the power of all things.

"The round form of the drum representing the universe," another example of the importance of the symbol of a circle. Not only was there a totality represented, but a source of power coming in the form of a drum beat.

The evening fires of Tiospaye would burn late into the night. The full moon made it seem like daylight and the dancing could go on forever. Never before was there such a feeling of confidence and freedom. From Sitting Bull's vision, they knew they were invincible. On the morning of the Custer Battle, June 25, 1876, the tribes were experiencing the restful slumber, sleeping in circles of harmony and peace.

Linda L. Stampoulos

The golden sun of a new day slowly pushes its brilliance into a waiting June morning. Mists of a cool night now meeting the warmth of dawn hang as if artistically draped by the Creator between the spirit world and mother earth. Photo is provided by the Denver Public Library, Western History Collection, Call Number X31212.

The Redemption of Black Elk

Flickering eerily across the landscape are the dying embers of the campfires of Tiospaye. It is quiet. It is peaceful. It is deceiving. Photo is provided by the Denver Public Library, Western History Collection, Call Number NS288.

The description of the morning continues: Majestic, regal, strong and stoic Sitting Bull stares ominously across the horizon on which land his people still peacefully and rhythmically slumber. One can only imagine the pain and grief and suffering within the holy man's heart as deep within he knows what others know not: it is the night not the dawn which lies ahead. It is the end not the beginning which the rising sun symbolizes on this June morning.

Off in the distance is the silent sound of thunder; not of the heavens but of earth; not of nature but of man. He hears not through his ears but through his spirit. Never again will his people gather and celebrate as they have just done. Never again will the freedom fires of Tiospaye burn so brightly among so many. It is dawn, but the time grows short. It is the day, but the night draws near. They will be victorious in the battle against Custer, but with that victory would come the last days of the scared hoop.

The tribe's sacred hoop was usually entrusted to the medicine man. Coming from a long line of these healers, Black Elk was very familiar with its power and meaning. In his 1896 report for the Smithsonian Institutes' Bureau of Ethnology entitled "The Ghost Dance Religion and the Sioux Outbreak of 1890" James Mooney stated that the medicine man of Big Foot's band carried such a hoop with him in their flight from the north, and displayed it at every dance held by the band until the fatal day of Wounded Knee.

Black Elk saw that outside elements were responsible for the breaking of the oneness and wholeness his people enjoyed. Large scale disruption began after the Indian victory at the Little Bighorn. However, Black Elk continued to believe the positive message of his vision. That there is not one hoop, but many hoops representing many nations and people of all colors. There is a promise of salvation for all people within the harmony of the sacred hoop. The challenge is to find a way to nourish the spiritual needs of a people while they search after their own uniqueness, their own identity in the modern world.

To continue our journey then, we must keep to Black Elk's message, concentrate on our own oneness, our own sacred hoop.

Pictured is a medicine lodge. It usually is the largest in the camp belonging to the medicine man. Here the Indians would congregate evenings to sing and dance. An elderly woman sits and rests. She is tanning a wolf skin. Photo is provided by the Denver Public Library, Western History Collection, Call Number X31654.

The Redemption of Black Elk

Pictured is Spotted Eagle, Medicine Man of the Itazipco Lakota. He holds his tribes hoop during the dance. Photo is provided by the Denver Public Library, Western History Collection, Call Number Z61.

Wicasa Ksapa Wakan Sica

Name your Heroes and your Demons

We have not even to risk the adventure alone for the heroes of all time have gone before us. The labyrinth is thoroughly known; we have only to follow the thread of the hero path, and where we had thought to travel outward, we shall come to the center of our own existence; where we had thought to be alone, we shall be with all the world.

> Joseph Campbell
> <u>The Hero With a Thousand Faces</u>

Linda L. Stampoulos

Name your Heroes and your Demons

Knowing we are not alone is a source of comfort as we continue to go through life. Our journey is made much easier knowing that someone else is there, sharing our joys and our sorrows. Sometimes it helps to think of those gone before, who traveled our same path and serve as models for our life.

Joseph Campbell often referred to the hero and the hero path. "A hero," he tells us, "is someone who has found something or done something beyond the normal range of achievement and experience. He has given his life to something bigger than himself." This, he explains, could be in terms of a physical deed, such as the brave acts of Crazy Horse; or, a spiritual deed, such as Black Elk's devotion to the fulfillment of his vision. But there is always a price to pay; the hero has sacrificed himself for the betterment of others.

Following the next footprint involves examination of the contents of your sacred hoop. While in your place of solitude and peace, you were asked to draw a circle containing your immediate concerns. Now you are to examine these concerns and determine whether they add to your life or take away from it. Keep in mind, your hoop contains both positive and negative elements: heroes and demons. This process of arranging the forces inside you compares to Jung's use of the *mandala*, the Sanskrit word meaning circle. He often would have his clients draw their mandala, and use it as an instrument of contemplation. Campbell tells us that the organizing of feelings and issues within the mandala is an instinctive expression of human desire to create organization from chaos and to address the confusing flux of inner and outer life.

You begin by placing your issues in some kind of order, always keeping the positive ones close and the negative ones toward the rim, away from the center. You are also asked to name them. Are they your heroes or your demons? "Naming" has a control power in itself. When casting out a demon, Jesus called it by name (Mark, Chapter 5). Identification reduces the perceived strength of the negative force and gives you more control over its power. It no longer can feed on your fear. In the same way, those positive forces become more prominent, giving you a strength you never realized you had. No one will ever be totally free from negative forces. There will always be demons invading our hoop. We must do our best to recognize them for what they represent, and keep them as far from our center as possible.

By repeating this exercise you will begin to become more and more aware of an unconsciousness that lies deep within. Visiting the quietness of your sacred place, drawing your hoop of containment limiting your concerns, the identification of your heroes and demons, are early steps toward self discovery. Each experience will bring increased inner strength because you are in control of the conflicting forces within each of us. Slowly the forces locked inside will emerge and you will position them within your sacred hoop. You are becoming coordinated with the greater consciousness of the universe. As Campbell says, "All that is unconscious is dangerous and powerful and must be controlled by consciousness. The hero transcends his humanity and reassociates himself with the powers of nature which are the true powers of our life and from which our mind removes us." Only through self discovery and meditation do we leave the distractions and worldly demands, and turn our sights inward, unlocking who we really are and what we really can become.

In his quest for the meaning of his mission, Black Elk would often rely on the heroes of his time. His cousin Crazy Horse was a source of inspiration for him. Crazy Horse was a true leader for his people. For a time he was a "shirt wearer," a kind of social servant who was responsible for the welfare of those members of his tribe, orphans, elders, who could not hunt or care for themselves. He also was a brave warrior and role model for young people. In the following meditative reading, Black Elk continues his account of the days following the Little Bighorn victory, and the capture and killing of his hero, Crazy Horse.

Meditative Reading

The Killing of Crazy Horse
The Death of a Hero

Black Elk tells of the days following the victory at the Little Bighorn, and the death of his cousin, Crazy Horse.

At about dark we were all ready so we went upstream on the Little Bighorn. We fled all night, following the battle at Greasy Grass Creek. By morning we reached a little dry creek and stopped here, making camp at once. We roasted some of our meat here and had a big feast. It was spotted with fat here and there. I wish I could have some now.

Then the next day we moved down the Rosebud to the place where the Rosebud goes through the high bluffs where we camped. We moved then downstream again as far as where we had had the sun dance and we wanted to see what the remains of the sun dance looked like. This was nothing but dirt all stirred up—the horses had just ruined everything. Reno had scouted through there and defiled it with the band of horses. Next we stopped at a sacred place where a big rock bluff was. The Indians claim that before the Custer fight the whole thing was pictured on it. Nobody could possibly get up to where the picture is. Things are foretold here always. When there was a man hanging down headfirst, why something will probably happen that year. And a year before the Custer fight there was a bunch of soldiers with their heads hanging down pictured on this bluff. Anything important that will happen that year will be pictured on this bluff. The rock is called Rock Writing Bluff. This rock stands right next to the water on the Rosebud. Here we camped and the drawing of the Custer fight was still there and the other people also saw it.

The next day the scattering of the people began. Crazy Horse's band started up Powder River to the Rocky Mountains. The Cheyenne moved westward toward the foot of the Bighorns. Crazy Horse's band encamped on Tongue River that fall. He had a fight with some Crows and brought back a lot of scalps. The Minneconjou came from Slim Buttes and stayed with Crazy Horse's that winter.

As I remember, the Minneconjou and Crazy Horse's band got together and tried to make peace with the whites. We sent some delegates to the soldiers to make peace with them.

Most of the time Crazy Horse was not in camp. On the road to Fort Robinson we found Crazy Horse all alone on a creek with just his wife. Crazy Horse said to my father: "Uncle, you might have noticed me, how I act, but it is for the good of my people that I am out alone. Out here I am making plans—nothing but good plans—for the good of my people. I don't care where the people go. They can go where they wish. There are lots of caves and this shows that I cannot be harmed." (There were things that he had to figure out and he was wanting the spirits to guide him. He would then go back to his people and tell them what he had learned.) "This country is ours, therefore I am doing this," said Crazy Horse.

We got back to Fort Robinson in about May. When we had stayed a few days, we heard that Crazy Horse and his band were coming. Red Cloud sent men out to escort him home. They met him at the buttes called Sits with the Young One also known as Pumpkin Buttes. There was a big council on and the people attended to honor Chief Crazy Horse.

They thought that Crazy Horse would have lots to say. The custom when going to war—the warrior ties up his horse's tail. Crazy Horse said: "This day I have untied my horse's tail and put my gun aside and I have sat down." This is all he said and he sat down. They wanted Crazy Horse to go back. He said: "Not until I rest, then I will be willing to go. But before I go give lots of ammunition to my people. I have set a place for my people that will be the reservation. The Black Hills belong to my people. I wish for my people to go there when I am gone."

During the winter, messengers had come to Crazy Horse's village from General Crook at Fort Robinson, promising amnesty if the Sioux would surrender and live on their reservation. My camp arrived in advance of the main village, probably about the first of May. Crazy Horse and nine hundred of his followers surrendered at Robinson on May 6, 1877.

In the evening of the next day after we got back to Red Cloud's Agency, some soldiers came there bringing Crazy Horse with them. He was riding his horse alone a little way ahead. They did not stay there long, but rode on over to the Soldiers' Town, and my father and I went along with many others to see what they were going to do.

When we got over there we could not see Crazy Horse, because there were soldiers and Lakota policemen all around where he was and people crowding outside.

In just a little while I could feel that something very bad was happening in there, and everybody was excited all at once, and you could hear voices buzzing all around. Then I heard a loud cry in our own language, and it said: "Don't touch me! I am Crazy Horse!" And suddenly something went through all the people there like a big wind that strikes all the trees at once. Somebody in there yelled something else, but everybody around me was asking or telling everybody he was sick, that he was hurt; and I was frightened, because everything felt the way it did that day when we were going up to kill on the Greasy Grass, and it seemed we all might begin fighting right away.

Then everything got quiet, and everybody seemed to be waiting for something. Then the people began to break up and move around, and I heard that Crazy Horse had just taken sick and maybe he would be alright soon. But it was not long until we all knew what had happened in there, because some of the people saw it happen, and I will tell you how it was.

They told Crazy Horse they would not harm him if he would go to the Soldiers' Town and have a talk with the Wasichu chief there. But they lied. They did not take him to the chief for a talk. They took him to the little prison with iron bars on the windows, for they had planned to get rid of him. And when he saw what they were doing, he turned around and took a little knife out of his robe and started out against those soldiers. Then Little Big Man, who had been his friend and was the one who told us boys that we were brave before my first fight when we attacked the wagons at War Bonnet Creek, took hold of Crazy Horse from behind and tried to get the knife away. And while they were struggling, a soldier ran a bayonet into Crazy Horse from one side at the back and he fell down and began to die. Then they picked him up and carried him into the soldier chief's office. The soldiers stood all around there and would not let anybody in and made the people go away. My father and I went back to our camp at Red Cloud Agency.

That night I heard mourning somewhere, and then there was more and more mourning, until it was all over the camp. Crazy Horse was dead; he was only about thirty-five years old. He was brave and good and wise. He never wanted anything but to save his people, and he fought the Wasichus only when they came to kill us in our own country. They could not kill him in battle. They had to lie to him and kill him that way. I cried all night, and so did my father.

When it was day, Crazy Horse's father and mother brought him over to our camp in a wagon. They put him in a box, and fastened the box on a travois, and went alone toward the east and north. I saw the two old people going away alone with their son's body. Nobody followed them. They went all alone, and I can see them going yet.

Linda L. Stampoulos

Above is a photoprint of an illustration from Frank Leslie's Illustrated Newspaper dated October 17, 1877. Pictured is a group Indian men and women following Crazy Horse's body as his parents begin the journey to his burial site near Camp Sheridan, Nebraska. This image is provided by the Denver Public Library, Western History Collection, Call Number X33723.

Talking Points

The Killing of Crazy Horse
The Death of a Hero

The forces within our hoop are constantly changing, that is why it is of critical importance that we take time everyday to assess these changes. When Black Elk experienced the loss of his cousin, he too had to make adjustments. He would often go into the Plains alone and contemplate all that was told to him. The Sacred Hoop of his vision not only allowed him to accept the death of Crazy Horse, it gave him hope for his own future. Crazy Horse was only a young man at the time of his death. Although he was not able to complete the full Circle of Winters, he still accomplished so many heroic deeds, upon reflection, gave Black Elk inspiration to continue his mission.

The Sacred Hoop as the Circle of Winters

In addition to our Sacred Hoop keeping us safe and contained, Black Elk tells us of another purpose. The colors making up the outside circle of the hoop explain our life journey, it is our circle of winters. Tracing the colors in a clockwise direction describes the stages we pass through as we grow old. When discussing the features of the circle Joseph Campbell points out that its own geometry indicates a journey. The line travels around going out and down and around back to where you started. It represents a total journey but on inspection has no beginning and no end.

Black Elk tells us, the South (red) is the source of life for the sun lives there. A man advances from there toward the setting sun of his life. As men and things grow older, they move toward the setting sun where all things pass. The West (black) is the greatest source of power, probably because as men get older they get wisdom. As they get older they approach the colder North (white) where the white hairs are. And does he not then arrive, if he lives, at the source of light and understanding which is the East (yellow), and completing the circle with the sun does he not return to where he began, to give back his life to all life, and his flesh to the earth whence it came.

He also tells us that when a man is born, he is four-legged. This means he crawls before he can walk. Then for years he is two-legged. He walks the earth strong and tall. In the end, he becomes three-legged, using a cane to help him complete his life journey.

Crazy Horse never completed a full circle of winters. Like many others during this tumultuous time, he was cut down in the prime of his life. The white miners and settlers were encroaching the Black Hills, and the U.S. Calvary was sent in to protect them.

A month after the Battle of the Little Bighorn, a Memorial Service was held for General George Armstrong Custer. Excerpts from the tributes given at the service appeared in the New York Times dated August of 1876:

> "I cannot wholly dissociate from my speaking thoughts of those noble brothers who fell on the same bloody field, a cordon of youth, beauty and strength. He gave over fourteen years of service defending his nation. These are surely pleasing incidents in the life of this hero-son, silver patches on the dark cloud that envelops that once happy life. And then comes rushing through the yet open windows of the soul the desolation that would reign in that far-off home, a

father's care, a mother's love, and then upward far above the arching sky, a silent prayer ascends to heaven, the spirit has gone to God who gave it."

Could these same words not be said if there had been a Memorial Service for Crazy Horse and those who died at the Little Bighorn? The pain of death and loss can be felt on both sides of a battle. But this battle held a much deeper consequence. The fame and reputation of Custer and his Seventh Calvary sparked a cause unlike anything before. The struggle to conquer the Frontier took on a much more passionate meaning. As the Excerpts continue:

"He responded to the call with that ardor of feeling and singleness of purpose that stamps his memory with lasting renown. Filled with a martial spirit and unmoved by danger, it is no wonder that his name among friends and foe should hold him in marked esteem. No wonder that those who contested the field against him and felt the powers of his uplifted arm are now asking the privilege of avenging his death."

After the Battle of the Little Bighorn, after the death of Crazy Horse, the tribes began to scatter. Black Elk and his family joined Sitting Bull and Gall and took refuge in Canada. Our journey continues as we look at the impact of the scattering of the people.

Linda L. Stampoulos

Joseph K. Dixon titled this photo "The Sacrament of Winter." Black Elk described the winter as very cold, and game was scare. Photo is provided by the Denver Public Library, Western History Collection, Call Number Z3156.

The Redemption of Black Elk

Pictured are Sitting Bull and members of his family. After the death of Crazy Horse, he and Gall and their followers took refuge in Canada. Photo is provided by the Denver Public Library, Western History Collection, Call Number X31936.

Cokatakiya

Find your Center

Expression of Self Harmony

My mandala is a cryptogram concerning the state of my self which is presented to me anew each day. In it I saw the self, that is, my whole being-actively at work...I had the distinct feeling that there was something central, and in time, I acquired through it a living conception of the self. Its basic motif is the premonition of a center of personality, a kind of central point within the psyche, to which is itself a source of energy. The energy of the central point is manifested in an almost irresistible compulsion and urge *to become what one is*, just as every organism is driven to assume the form that is characteristic of its nature, no matter what the circumstances. Although the center is represented by an innermost point, it is surrounded by a periphery containing everything that belongs to the self, the paired opposites that make up the total personality.

Carl Gustav Jung
The Archetypes and the Collective Unconscious

Find your Center

After the Battle of the Little Bighorn, the tribes were being hunted down and made to relocate onto reservation land. Those who resisted scattered and hid. During this time, the people had to abandon their customary way of life; no longer could they play their drums, sing, dance, and make camp to care for the elders and the very young. Those elements that were the strength of their life were forced underground. Imagine the distance the sound of a drum could travel. Their heartbeat had been silenced and many were forced to take refuge in Canada.

The scattering of the people is a perfect example of a loss of focus, a loss of the centering of a people. On an individual level, Black Elk spoke often of the importance of the sacred hoop and in particular, its center.

The first sections of this book encourage you to coordinate and order the forces that affect you everyday. It was recommended that you place the negative forces as far away as possible, close to the rim of your hoop. This process prevents them from gaining access to the energy of the center, the source of psychic power. Prior to the positioning the issues within your hoop you had to determine if they were positive or negative. The more positive the force, the closer it was placed to your center.

But this is where the thought process and the mind's influence end. Campbell reminds us that the brain is a secondary organ and must not put itself in control. It must submit to serve the humanity of the body. As one reaches his true center, the mind's involvement in assigning a value to the issue is no longer at work, neither positive nor negative forces prevail. Arrival at the true center establishes a psychic connection to something greater than one's self. A stream of energy runs through the center, axis mundi, from bottom to top. The whirlpool of positive and negative forces continue to spin around inside the hoop, but the individual who has found his center leaves his thought process behind and begins to feel what Campbell calls the "thou" feeling of life.

Once you find your center, it becomes a source of psychic energy, you become one in accord with the inevitability of your life. You begin to live with a knowledge of life's mystery, giving you a zest and a new balance. As your anxieties begin to ease, you will see the positive values becoming more clear. Unless your center is found, you are torn apart. You listen closer to the system that dominates you than to yourself.

We are so accustomed to living within the rules of a system. The demands of which, Campbell tells us, can eat you up and cause you to lose your humanity. Although we can't always change the system, he advises us to find a way to live within the system as a human being. We do this, he says, by resisting the system's impersonal claims. If a person doesn't listen the needs of his own spiritual and heart life and insist on a certain program, the person has aligned himself with a programmatic life, one that his body is not interested in at all.

Jung tells us that in the center of the circle there is a conscious self-awareness and balance. He says that every person has an innate tendency to pursue this inner harmony which aligns the conscious with the personal unconscious in a psychic connection.

Have you ever experienced a psychic connection? It is a connection to something bigger than yourself. You may have experienced it and never realized what it was. Often this connection or communication comes through the senses. It could be the feeling that comes when you are walking on a beach, feeling the power of the wind, or experiencing the smell of something that triggers a lost memory. It leaves you with a feeling of a connection, a yielding acknowledgment of something that has gone before and yet continues to present itself as a dominant force. This joins you with the collective power of those who have gone before and those not yet born. For Black Elk this experience occurred during the thunderstorms and also during the dance. It began with the Sun Dance and eventually lead to the Ghost Dance. In the next reading he tells of the years with Sitting Bull and Gall.

Meditative Reading

Retreat to Canada with Sitting Bull and Gall The Scattering of the People

I recalled my vision now and then and wondered when my duty was to come. This winter we moved up to Canada with Sitting Bull and Gall. We stayed over here all winter and then it came spring. I am now fifteen years old. We were still in Canada yet. That June 1878, Sitting Bull and Gall had a sun dance at the Forest Butte in Canada.

In his narrative of the Sioux Outbreak, James Mooney details the following:

> Being pursued by General Terry, Sitting Bull and his band made their escape northward into Canada, where they remained until 1881, when he surrendered, through the mediation of the Canadian authorities, on a promise of pardon. To obtain subsistence while in Canada, his people had been obliged to sell almost all they possessed, including their firearms, so that they returned to their old homes in an impoverished condition.

Black Elk continues his account:

We were camping in Canada still. My father and I went out hunting from Clay Creek to Little River Creek where we camped. We had nothing to eat now because it was winter and we did not see any game of any sort. That night we got very hungry and it was in cold weather. It looked as though we might starve to death if we did not find some game soon, and everybody was downhearted. We fixed up a little place so that we could build a fire in it. While I was lying there in a bison robe a coyote began to howl not far off, and suddenly I knew it was saying something. It was not making words, but it said something plainer that words: "Two-legged one, on this ridge west of you over there are buffalo. Beforehand you shall see two more two-legged people." I told my father: "Father, you heard that coyote howl-that coyote said there are buffalo on that ridge west of us, but before you shall see two two-leggeds. So father, let us rise early."

By this time my father noticed I had some odd power, and he believed me. It was very cold and it was snowing. Before we came to the ridge, we saw two horses, dim in the blowing snow beside some bushes. They were huddled up with their tails to the wind and their heads hanging low. When we came closer, there was a bison robe shelter in the brush, and in it were an old man and a boy, very cold and hungry and discouraged. They were Lakota and glad to see us, but they were feeling weak, because they were out two days and saw nothing but snow. We camped here with them in their shelter in the brush. We all got on top of the ridge and looked all around. We could see miles and miles but no sign of buffalo. We waited in the shelter for the snow haze to open so we could see again. Suddenly the snow haze opened and we saw a shaggy bull's head coming out of the blowing snow. Then seven more appeared. They could not see us and were drifting with the wind so they could not smell us.

We stood up and made vows to the four quarters of the world saying: "Haho, haho." Then we got our horses from the brush and came around to where the bison would pass as they drifted with the wind. The two old men were to shoot first and then we two boys would follow on horseback. The men crept up and shot, but they were so cold, and maybe excited that they only got one bison. They cried "Hoka!" and we boys charged after the other bison. They had only one buffalo and we pursued the rest. The snow was blowing all the while and the buffalo just turned around and took back track and the snow being broken, it was much easier for the horses to follow them back. I got off my horse and took my gun shot four buffalo. The gun froze on my hand in no time and the other fellow tried to help me get the gun loose from my hand. After the gun was off, I took snow and began to rub my hands with it.

When we had too much meat to carry home, we usually cache it. We spent the next day butchering the meat, and divided it evenly. The meat was not frozen but when it was put on the horses it began to freeze. We camped once that day and we kept on going, and at about sundown we got back to the village. The people were glad to see us with all that meat.

The morning after we reached the village I went out to look for our horses that were in a draw where there was cottonwood, and five of them had frozen to death. The cold was very bad after the wind stopped blowing. We began to feel homesick for our own country where we used to be happy. The old people talked much about it and the good days before the trouble came.

Nothing of much importance happened here. We broke camp in the spring of 1880. All of our horses had died and most of us had to travel on foot. There were six men and two women in this party besides myself. The whole following year I forgot all about my vision. We started back to the United States because we were tired of being in Canada. There was a medicine man named Chased by Spiders who was with us. We came to All Gone Tree Creek. There was timber there but the soldiers cut it away; that is why it was called that name. This was right close to Poplar, Montana.

The Assiniboines started home now and brought us many presents and lots of things to eat. The next day we went back to the Assiniboines' agency where the Indians gave us plenty more to eat. From the Fort Peck agency, at Poplar River, Montana, we headed down stream.

When I came back my people seemed to be in poverty. Before I went some of my people were looking well, but when I got back they all looked pitiful. There had been quite a famine.

This fall I heard that there were some men named Kicking Bear, Short Bull, and Bear Comes Out had gone and seen the Messiah. It was toward the west right around Idaho somewhere. There was a sacred man there. These three men had gone to see the sacred man and they came back that following fall and reported that they had seen the Messiah and actually talked to him and that he had given them some sacred relics. These three men had brought some sacred red and white paint that the sacred man had given them. This paint was broken up into little pieces and distributed among the people.

These people told me that these men had actually seen the Messiah and that he had given them these things. They should put this paint on and have a ghost dance.

The Redemption of Black Elk

Pictured are five men, possibly members of Big Foot's band, taken at Pine Ridge, South Dakota. Photo is provided by the Denver Public Library, Western History Collection, Call Number NS187.

Linda L. Stampoulos

Oglala Sioux dancers perform the Sun Dance on the Pine Ridge Reservation, South Dakota. Photo is provided by the Denver Public Library, Western History Collection, Call Number X31670.

Talking Points

Retreat to Canada with Sitting Bull and Gall
The Scattering of the People

The retreat to Canada was short-lived. The people missed their homeland and slowly Black Elk, Sitting Bull and their people returned. One by one they began to obey the soldiers and move on to the reservation lands. Their way of life totally changed and they became dependent on the White government for food. They signed treaties that guaranteed them food and other provisions. However, the promises were not kept.

In his report to the Assistant Adjutant-General, Captain J. H. Hurst, Fort Bennett, South Dakota, listed the Indian complaints. Among their grievances the Indians stated that the game had been destroyed and driven out by the White people; that their children were taken from them to eastern schools and kept for years; that the issue of their annuity goods was delayed so late in the winter as to cause much suffering; and that they were expected to plow the land and raise grain when the climate would not permit. His report goes on to state that these issues are well founded and justified by facts.

Reservation life was forced upon them and the Indians, who for their entire lives hunted and followed the buffalo, were now struggling to reconcile themselves to the ways of a new civilization. Hungry, desperate and depressed, Black Elk and his people searched in vain for a center, a focus for their lives. He said, "At that time I could see that the hoop was broken and all scattered out and I thought, I am going to try my best to get my people back into the hoop again."

Then came news of a messiah, a Paiute named Wovoka was teaching about a new religion called the Ghost Dance.

Kicking Bear initiated the first Ghost Dance on the Rosebud and Pine Ridge Reservations. Later he went to Standing Rock by invitation of Sitting Bull to inaugurate the dance on that reservation.

Black Elk was excited about this new dance and traveled to Manderson to watch them dance. He saw that it had many of the elements shown to him in his vision. Participants danced in a circle, and in the center was a cottonwood tree. As Black Elk tells us, "they had a sacred pole in the center. It was a circle in which they were dancing and I could clearly see that this was my sacred hoop and in the center they had an exact duplicate of my tree that never blooms and it came to my mind that perhaps with this power the tree would bloom and the people would get into the sacred hoop again." Black Elk found a connection, and perhaps, an opportunity to fulfill the message of his vision given to him so many years before.

Often it is at times of utter despair that we turn inward and find the energy of our center, times when it is least expected and thought impossible. But somehow the energy is tapped, and individuals accomplish the most amazing things.

One might say that the Ghost Dance became everyone's last chance at returning hope in these desperate times. Not being able to change the system, the people had found a way to find their center and yet live within the system, just as Campbell recommended we do. They even agreed to only dance a few times a week. But their intense celebration and the promise of a return to the old ways posed a great threat to the soldiers.

Giving hope, providing a path does empower us. Whether it be on an individual level, or as is the case of Black Elk, on a tribal level, the energizing forces are the same. By connecting to those "ghosts" or that spirit army who has gone before, we have them return to join the effort, to recapture dreams, and to ignite the beacons that were dying. Once again Black Elk's footprints rise up to show us a way, a path toward inner power. A path that leads from "the place where crying begins," to a land where the buffalo again roam free and eagles soar high above the rainbow door.

Linda L. Stampoulos

Pictured Sitting Bull on trial at Standing Rock Agency, North Dakota, for allegedly instigating the Crow to go to war. Many members of his band gathered around the three men sitting behind table who are (left to right): Colonel Townsend, 12th Infantry; Colonel Barrister (gray derby hat); and Commissioner James McLaughlin. McLaughlin was appointed by President Chester A. Arthur on October 27, 1881 to oversee Standing Rock Agency. McLaughlin fostered rifts between Sitting Bull, Gall and others to lessen Sitting Bull's influence with the Indians. Photo is provided by the Denver Public Library, Western History Collection, Call Number B751.

The Redemption of Black Elk

Three leaders of the Ghost Dance, are pictured outside a building in front of a covered wagon, Pine Ridge Agency, South Dakota. Left to right are: Chief Kicking Bear, who wears a breechcloth, tunic and vest with his blanket on the ground; Chief Young Man Afraid of His Horses, and Standing Bear who is holding a ceremonial pipe. Kicking Bear was reported to be the "chief high priest of the Ghost Dance among the Sioux," and by invitation of Sitting Bull, inaugurated the dance on the Standing Rock Reservation. Photo is provided by the Denver Public Library, Western History Collection, Call Number X31367.

Can Wakan

Nourish the Sacred Tree

Let me tell you why we consider the cottonwood tree to be so very sacred:

Long ago it was the cottonwood who taught us how to make our tipis, for the leaf of the tree is an exact pattern of the tipi. Another reason why we chose the cottonwood tree to be at the center of our lodge is that the Great Spirit has shown us that, if you cut an upper limb of this tree crosswise, there you will see in the grain a perfect five pointed star, which, to us, represents the presence of the Great Spirit. This will be the sacred Morning Star who stands between the darkness and the light, and who represents knowledge. Also perhaps you have noticed that even in the very lightest breeze you can hear the voice of the cottonwood tree; this we understand is its prayer to the Great Spirit, for not only men, but all things and all beings pray to Him continually in differing ways.

Black Elk to Joseph Epes Brown
<u>The Sacred Pipe</u>

Linda L. Stampoulos

Nourish the Sacred Tree

Black Elk continually referenced the Sacred Tree of his vision, and emphasized its need to be nourished. He knew that people had to connect with their inner self and learn of its dimension. The true person waiting to be discovered, had to be found. What's more, it had to be encouraged to grow and blossom. This is not an easy task. It takes a courage of conviction, one easily forfeited to the demands of this world.

Recently there was an Associated Press article describing the attempts of the New Jersey Masons to obtain more members. "We're not a secret society," claimed the Grand Master, "we're an organization with some secrets." So it was with the members of the Sioux Nation, still in exile. They held tightly to the "old ways" and because they presented a threat to the encroaching numbers of White settlers, they too had to be an "organization with some secrets."

One of the most compelling secrets or forces that emerged was the word of a Messiah; a leader who could reclaim their culture and set them free from the captive oppression facing them on the Reservations. Rumors spread telling the story of Wovoka, a Paiute, whose visions served as an inspiration to those who yearned for freedom. Stories spread of his ability to perform miracles and even raise men from the dead. He combined Christianity with Paiute mysticism to form the Ghost

Dance Religion.

His teachings provided a means for the people to get in touch with who they really wanted to be. By believing Wovoka's teachings, the people began to experience a return of values and spirit. The metaphor of the "tree" epitomized the renaissance that was about to begin. Everyone felt it; everyone believed it.

The tree was in the center of their dance, and was nourished by the energy of their center. Its direction of strength ran from bottom to top connecting with the forces and energy of the center. It was *waken*, sacred, and it held a place of high honor. The cottonwood tree was always chosen for the center of the dance, including the Sun Dance.

The custom of a circle dance centering around a tree is common to other cultures. In parts of Germany, May 1st is an especially important day. In German villages, it has been the custom for centuries to cut a tall and straight tree, the Maibaum (May Tree), a day or two before May 1 and place it in the middle of the village. It was decorated with a wreath of Spring flowers and colorful ribbons. The traditional Maypole dance has an even number of dancers facing alternatively clockwise and counterclockwise, they move in a circle in the direction they are facing raising and passing the ribbons they hold. The elements are always the same across cultures, a celebration, a dance in a circle, and a tree in the center.

Joseph Campbell tells us that the symbol of the tree is present in many religions. Christ died on the tree of the cross and was born to the spirit; and the Buddha sits under the tree of knowledge and immortal life. The imagery gives one the realization that there is a higher plain and the body is a vehicle. It is clear to Campbell that Black Elk's vision was part of a "shamanic experience." For the shaman, all that exists in the revealed world has a living force within it. This life energy force is conceived as a divine force which permeates all. The knowledge that life is power is the realization of the shaman.

Another interpretation of the imagery of the tree and the mystery of the shaman is presented by Joan Halifax. From their visions and dreams, shamans describe a "cosmic tree" which is a symbol of perpetual regeneration. It is this tree with its life-giving waters that binds all realms together, the roots of the tree penetrate the depths of the Underworld. The body of the tree transects the Middle World, and the crown embraces the heavens. This great tree stands at the very center of the universe directing the vision of a culture skyward towards the eternally sacred.

On an individual level, the tree represents a person's potential, coming from the center, it is the true core of their life's purpose. Nourishing it and helping it "bloom" becomes a process of self-realization, coming in touch with the real meaning and intent of one's life. For Black Elk's people, the Ghost Dance Religion promised a return to the old ways; an opportunity for the individual to return to a place of pride, a place where they could again feel good about themselves. In the Meditative Reading that follows, Black Elk gives his account of the Ghost Dance and the tragedy that followed.

Meditative Reading

The Ghost Dance Religion and the Wounded Knee Massacre
Blood Spills on the Sacred Tree

Black Elk describes the search for the Messiah and his involvement in the Ghost Dance Religion. He describes the Wounded Knee Massacre.

People told me that these men, Kicking Bear, Short Bull, and Bear Comes Out had actually seen the Messiah and that he had given them the relics. They should put this paint on and have a Ghost Dance, and in doing this they would save themselves, that there is another world coming—a world just for the Indians. But if you want to get into this other world, you would have to have this paint on. It should be put all over the face and head, and that this Ghost Dance would draw them to this other world and that the whites would have no power. In this other world there was plenty of meat—just like olden times—every dead person was alive again and all the buffalo that had been killed would be over there again roaming around. This world was to come like a cloud. This painting and Ghost Dance would make everyone get on the red road again. Everyone was eager to get back to the red road again.

This sacred man (Wovoka, the Ghost Dance Messiah) had presented two eagle feathers to one of these three men. The sacred man had said to him: "Receive these eagle feathers and behold them, for my father will cause these two eagle feathers to bring your people back to him." This is all that was heard the whole winter. At first when I heard this I was bothered, because my vision was nearly like it and it looked as though my vision were really coming true and that if I helped, probably with my power that I had that I could make the tree bloom and that I would get my people back into that sacred hoop again where they would prosper. This was in my mind. I wanted to see this man personally and find out and it was setting firmer in my mind every day.

These fellows came home in the spring of 1890. I heard that at the head of Cheyenne Creek, north of Pine Ridge, Kicking Bear had held the first Ghost Dance. From the rumors and gossips I heard that this Messiah was the son of the Great Spirit that had come out there. Then the next thing I heard was that they were dancing below Manderson on Wounded Knee. I wanted to find out things, because it was setting strongly in my heart and something seemed to tell me to go and I resisted it for quite awhile but then I could no longer resist, so I got on my horse and went to this Ghost Dance near Manderson and watched them dance.

They had a sacred pole in the center. It was a circle in which they were dancing and I could clearly see that this was my sacred hoop and in the center they had an exact duplicate of my tree that never blooms and it came to my mind that perhaps with this power the tree would bloom and the people would get into the sacred hoop again. It seemed that I could recall all my vision in it. The more I thought about it, the stronger it got in my mind. Furthermore, the sacred articles that had been presented were scarlet relics and their faces were painted red. They had that pipe and the eagle feathers. It was all from my vision. So I sat there and felt sad. Then happiness overcame me all at once and it got hold of me right there. I was to be intercessor for my people and yet I was not doing my duty. Perhaps it was this Messiah that had pointed me out and he might have set this to remind me to get to work again to bring my people back into the hoop and the old religion.

Again I recalled Harney Peak in the Black Hills, the center of the earth. And I remembered my vision that the spirits had said to me: "Boy, take courage, they shall take you to the center of the earth." When they took me here, they said: "Behold all the universe, the good things of the earth. All this behold it, because they shall be your own." Then I saw people prospering all over. And I recalled my six grandfathers. They told me through their power I would be intercessor on earth for my people. They had told me that I should know everything so therefore I made up my mind to join them. What I went there first for was to find out what they had heard, but now I changed my mind and was going there to use my own power to bring the people together. The dance was finished for that day, but the next day there was to be another dance, so I stayed all night for another one.

Just then I happened to think of my father and my sister and brothers which I had lost the year before, I couldn't keep the tears from running out of my eyes and so I put my head up to keep the tears from running out. I was really sorry and cried with my whole heart. The more I cried, the more I could think about my people. They were in despair. I thought about my vision and that my people should have a place in this earth where they would be happy every day and that their nation might live, but they had gone on the wrong road and they had gone into poverty but they would be brought back into the hoop. Under the tree that never bloomed I stood and cried because it faded away. I cried and asked the Great Spirit to help me to make it bloom again. I could not stop crying no matter how much I tried.

Then I had a funny feeling of shivering all over my body and this showed that it really was the real thing. Everyone knew my power and with my own will to make that tree bloom, I joined the people there.

At this time there was quite a famine among the people and some of them really believed in this Messiah and were hoping that this land of promise would come soon so that they would be through with the poverty. Many of them wanted to know more about this. I told my vision through songs. The fourth time I sang it there people all began to cry, because the white man had taken our world from us and we were like prisoners of war.

I was leader in every dance. Soon I had developed so much power that even if I would stand in the center of the circle and wave this red stick, the people would fall into swoons without dancing and see their visions. (Black Elk was considered one of the chief Ghost Dancers.)

The ghost shirt was to be worn in the Ghost Dances. So I started the ghost shirt. I made the first two shirts according to what I saw in the vision. The first one I made was for Afraid of Hawk, and I made another one for the son of Big Road. These shirts were considered to be bullet-proof.

Some chiefs came over from Pine Ridge to White Clay Creek north of Pine Ridge—Fire Thunder, Little Wound, and Young American Horse. These men brought a message in behalf of the soldiers that this matter of the Ghost Dance should be looked into, that there should be rulings over it, but they did not mean to take the dance away from us. We were dancing nearly every day and I heard that this is what the agent said to the people. He had made a ruling that we should dance three days every month and during the rest of the time we should go out and make a living of some kind for ourselves. This was all he said to them. When these men brought the news back, we were all satisfied with it and we agreed to do it.

Early in the morning the crier announced that we would have a meeting with the Brules. When the people got together this is what I told them: "My relatives, there is a certain thing that we have done. From that certain sacred thing we have done, we have had visions. In our visions we have seen and we have also heard that our relatives that have gone before us are actually in the Promised Land and that we are also going there. They are with the Wanekia. So therefore the Wasichu if they want to, they may fight us, and if they fight us, if we are going to we will win; so have in your minds a strong desire and take courage. We must depend upon the departed ones who are in the Promised Land that is coming and who are with the Wanekia. We should remember this. Because in the first place our grandfather has set the two-leggeds on earth with the power of where the sun goes down."

We moved camp to the Cheyenne River north of Pine Ridge. Most of the Oglalas were camping around Pine Ridge. I was looking out for horses and when I returned I learned that two policemen had come after me to be on their side as a scout. Two days later I learned that the soldiers (the Seventh Calvary) were marching toward Wounded Knee. This was in the month of the Popping Trees—December. I heard that Big Foot was coming from a young man who had come there. Rough Feather I heard was going to get Big Foot, who was coming from his camp near the mouth of the Medicine Root Creek on White River. At that time there were some soldiers camping somewhere around there on the other side of the river.

Rough Feather went over there to get Big Foot. He wanted them to come in a south-easterly direction, but they did not do it. They wanted to follow up Medicine Root. Big Foot's camp came to the creek of Porcupine Butte where the soldiers met them and they nearly had a fight here. The soldiers brought Big Foot back to Wounded Knee. That evening the soldiers gathered around where they had camped. The soldiers had them well guarded all night.

It was December 29, 1890, the next morning. They carried

Big Foot over to the officers, for he was sick. They told the rest of Big Foot's people to bring their guns over there. Everyone stacked their guns and even their knives up in the office at the officers' Headquarters. The soldiers were searching all the tipis for weapons. There were two men near Big Foot's tipi who wore blankets made out of white sheets, with just their eyes showing. Some of them had probably hidden their knives. The officer who was taking the guns from them went up to those men and pulled their white blankets apart and one of them had his gun concealed inside the sheet. He proceeded to the other one and opened it and just as he was going to get his gun, this man shot him. This man's name was Yellow Bird. This fellow did not want to give up his gun , and did not intend to shoot the white man at all—the gun just went off. Of course the soldiers were all around there already with their wagon guns on the hill north, across the flat east, and across the creek. The Indian scouts were behind the soldiers on the south. Yellow Bird and the white officer were wrestling with his gun and they had rolled down together on the ground and were wrestling with it. Dog Chief was right there when they took the guns and was standing right by these men while wrestling. This man was a friend of mine and he saw the whole thing.

    Big Foot was the first Indian that was killed by an officer before the wagon guns began to shoot. They had carried Big Foot over to where the guns were being given up and immediately after the shooting of Yellow Bird the officer shot Big Foot. Yellow Bird went into a tipi nearby and killed lots of them probably before he died. The Indians all ran to the stacks of guns and got their guns during a lull while the soldiers were loading again. A soldier ran up to tear the tipi away to get at Yellow Bird but the latter shot at them as they came up and killed them. They fired at the tipi and the soldiers' guns set it afire and he died in there.

The Redemption of Black Elk

The night before this I was over in the camp at Pine Ridge and I couldn't sleep. When I saw the soldiers going out it seemed that I knew there would be trouble. I was walking around all night until daylight. After my meal early that morning I got my horse and while I was out I heard shooting over to the east; I heard wagon guns going off. This was a little distance from the camp and when I heard this gun I felt it right in my body, so I went out and drove the horses back to the camp for I knew there was trouble. Just as I got back with the horses there was a man who returned from Pine Ridge and had come back because he had heard this.

I just thought it over and I thought I should not fight. I doubted about this Messiah business and therefore it seemed that I should not fight for it, but anyway I was going because I had already decided to. If I turned back the people would think it odd, so I just decided to go anyway. There were now over twenty of us going. As we neared there was a horseback coming toward us. He said: "Hey, hey, hey, they have murdered them!" Just then right before us I could see a troop of soldiers coming down a canyon. They stopped their horses and asked me what to do, so we decided we'd first see what we could do and then we'd do it. We started out and at the head of the gulch we went along the creek and got on top of the hill at the head of the gulch now called Battle Creek.

In the morning when the battle started, I could hear the shooting from Pine Ridge. With about twenty other young men, I started out to defend my people. When we got on the hill at the head of the draw about two and one half miles west of the monument, we could see some Indians being captured by two small troops of soldiers. This was at the head of the draw. I could hear the cannons and rifles going off down there and I could see soldiers all over the hills on each side of the draw. Then I said to the men whom I had led there: "Take courage, these are our relatives. We shall try to take the captives back. Furthermore, our women and children are lying dead. Think about this and take courage."

I had good eyes at this time and I could see cavalrymen scattered all over the hills. After I had said this to my young men I proceeded down on horseback and they followed me. Right by the yellow pine in the head of the gulch there was an Indian wounded through the legs by the name of Little Finger. Another man was following me, Iron White Man, and we put this wounded man behind him on his horse. At the very end of the gulch this wounded man fell off. Then another Indian came along and we asked him to take him over to a safe place. We took him across the hills northwest to safety. At the head of the gulch I saw a baby all alone. It was adopted by my wife's father. Its name was Blue Whirlwind. I was going to pick her up but I left her for she was in a safe place.

We started north toward where the horses are and we stopped right this side of the horses. We started out straight north under the first white clay spot a little ways up the hill. To the north was a troop of cavalry and about one hundred yards to the east was another troop of soldiers by the pine trees. Two of my men went to where the captives were and there was another Indian riding a black horse standing right this side of the captives.

Just as the two men got to where the soldiers were and got to where the black horse rider was standing, the farthest troop over there fired on us first and shot right across the draw as we retreated. Then after a little bit the main body of the men said: "Take courage, it is time to fight!" As the cavalrymen fired, the horses stampeded across the hills here.

We went back to Pine Ridge just after dark. It was about fifteen miles by the old road. When the soldiers gathered on the hill they began to go back on that ridge over there. After the soldiers did their dirty work over there they began to march up Wounded Knee. The soldiers wanted to fight yet, but we did not care so much about charging them. I wanted to see the place where Big Foot and his people got killed and as I followed down the draw I could see men and women lying dead all along there. Soldiers and Indians afterwards were here and there.

The day was cold even though it was sunny. That night the snow covered us and we all almost died from the cold. As I went down toward the village, I could see children dying all over—it was just a sight. I did not get as far as Big Foot's body though. I thought I would probably die before this thing was over and I just figured that there would be a day when I could either take revenge or die.

The people fled downstream and we followed them down. They camped below a stream with no tipis, they were just sitting by their fires. I went among them and I heard my mother singing a death song for me. Mother was glad to see me, as she thought I died over there.

I got up at daybreak. This morning war parties went out to Pine Ridge to fight. So I got on my horse and right there a buckskin rider went past me, his name was Protector. I went up the hill and they began to shoot at me. I turned and fled toward the hill and I could hear the bullets hitting my clothes. Then something hit me on the belt on the right side. My doubt and fear for the moment killed my power and during that moment I was shot.

Protector ran up and grabbed me for I was falling off my horse. He tore his blanket up and wrapped it around my wound. Then Protector told me to go home and said, "You must not die today, you must live, for the people depend on you."

Linda L. Stampoulos

Talking Points

The Ghost Dance Religion and the Wounded Knee Massacre Blood Spills on the Sacred Tree

Wovoka's teachings promised the Indians that they would again rise to power and with the help of the dead, they would reclaim the land; the buffalo would return, and they would be free. He promised all these things would come to pass in a short time; however, the religion must be kept a secret from the White people. Special investigations were ordered to "get to the bottom" of this Ghost Dance movement and the potential Sioux uprising. Like so many other events in history, it was viewed as a "movement" rather than accepted as a religion, and tragedy was near at hand.

On December 15, 1890, Sitting Bull was killed while resisting arrest on the Standing Rock Reservation. Couriers were sent after the fleeing Indians warning them to return to the agency, where they would be safe, or suffer the consequences if found outside the reservation. Within a few days, many had come in and surrendered.

The only prominent leader outside of the Bad Lands who was considered dangerous was Big Foot, whose village was at the mouth of Deep Creek. Big Foot and his band of Minneconjous had fled from the Cheyenne River Reservation on December 23rd to take refuge in the Bad Lands. They were alarmed at the news of Sitting Bull's death and feared the soldiers. Orders had been given to Major Whitside of the Seventh Calvary to intercept Big Foot's party in its flight. On December 28th, Big Foot raised a white flag, and asked for a meeting. Major Whitside refused and demanded an

The Redemption of Black Elk

unconditional surrender, which at once was given, and the Indians moved on with the troops to Wounded Knee Creek. In order to make the assurance complete, four additional troops of the Seventh Calvary were added to make a total force of 470 men, as against a total of 106 warriors then present in Big Foot's band. The rest is history.

Black Elk's account of the tragedy that ensued is accurate. The souls lost in the bloody snow will forever stand as a reminder of their last effort to hold on to the old ways and live as they did for centuries. But for Black Elk, the hope for his people did not end at Wounded Knee. In his lament he called for *Wakan Tanka* to cause their spirits to rise up from the bloody snow and help the tree to bloom again.

This metaphorical footprint that Black Elk talks about is cloaked in the people's despair. His prayer for them is one that asks for the realization of hope and a return to the old ways, the culture and the value system that was, in fact, their life. Linkages between the metaphor of the Sacred Tree and Black Elk's pathway to inner strength come in the reflection of Maslow's hierarchy of needs. Maslow begins with a description of the primary physical needs: food, water, shelter, common to everyone. All of these are rather basic and yet necessary for each individual. He goes on to present stages that develop into more complex needs. It is upon examination of Maslow's higher levels of need that we discover a connection to Black Elk's next footprint and his dream for his people. Self-realization and those needs leading up to it: self-respect, confidence, achievement, independence, and freedom comprise the "nourishment" Black Elk prayed for to help the tree to bloom again.

Campbell tells us that the realization of these esteem needs guides us inward to our "bliss station," a place of peace and self-realization. This is a place where we can develop a discipline for pulling all those scattered aspects of ourselves and putting an order to them. Upon continually returning to our sacred place we eventually rise up to a higher platform, a higher spiritual plain. The forces of society may try to lower our sights, but once there is a realization of who we are in this place, there is an explosion of self-worth and higher consciousness. We begin to live in terms of who we believe we are, not who or what society tells us we should be.

Black Elk's reference to the Daybreak Star is another strong connection to the nourishment of the Sacred Tree. In his vision, Black Elk learned that this star, also called the Morning Star, shines brightest before sunrise. It signifies the desire for and the certainty of more light to come. He tells us that he awakes about the same time everyday, the time the Morning Star rises, for knowledge and wisdom come to those who rise to see it. The people should say, "Behold the star of wisdom." Recalling his description of the cut cottonwood branch, "you will see in the grain a perfect five-pointed star." The star offers a promise to those who gaze upon it. The promise that more light will certainly come. For those who believe Black Elk's words, wisdom and understanding will also follow. The understanding of who you are and what you might become. This takes us to the final footprint on our path to inner strength: the road we must choose to follow.

The Redemption of Black Elk

Chief Kicking Bear speaks from inside the council circle on the Pine Ridge Reservation, South Dakota. He and his people discuss what they should do to continue to survive after Wounded Knee. Photo is provided by the Denver Public Library, Western History Collection, Call Number X31474.

Linda L. Stampoulos

Chief Hump, a Minnicoujou, is pictured with members of his family. He fought on Calhoun Hill at the Little Bighorn with Crazy Horse and Gall, where he received a bullet wound in his leg. It was reported that Kicking Bear began his Ghost Dance at the camps of Hump and Big Foot. According to Mooney, Hump was the most dangerous leader of dissatisfaction on the Cheyenne River Reservation after the death of Sitting Bull. However, he worked well with General Miles and brought his band of 400 people into Fort Bennett and complied with the orders of surrender. He subsequently rendered valuable service for peace. He later he became a U.S. Scout. Photo is provided by the Denver Public Library, Western History Collection, Call Number X31816.

Canku Luta Ogna Mani

Walk the Red Road

Long before the first satellite circled the globe, the great Oglala Holy Man Black Elk was given a vision. He said he was taken out into space to look down on the earth, and in so doing, he knew that it was holy. When you look at the earth from space, you know Black Elk was right, that the whole universe is our tabernacle. Indigenous people *feel* that the earth is our grandmother. She lives.

Black Elk was led down the path blazed by Red Cloud, Crow Dog, Crazy Horse, Sitting Bull, and others of their generation. I feel that Black Elk's purpose was to preserve our nation's sacred tree of life. I believe the last root of our tree still lives, just enough to regenerate the tree, and with it, our people's spiritual survival.

I believe my life should serve as an example for those who will follow Black Elk's path after I depart for the spirit world. I want Indian youth to take heart, to have faith. I want them to know that the Great Mystery is there for everyone and has a path for them. It is not strict and narrow. It winds and twists and branches off in every direction, but as long as they follow it freely and respectfully, it will take them where they are meant to go.

Russell Means
Yankton and Oglala band of the Lakota Sioux

Walk the Red Road

"Behold the earth, for across it there are two roads"

With these words, the fourth grandfather in Black Elk's great vision told of the two roads in life that a person can choose between. The black road (also called blue) is a fearful road that runs from where the sun shines continually to where the sun goes down (east and west), and it is the road of the Thunder-beings. "Behold the black road for it shall be a fearful road. With this road you shall defend yourself."

He went on to say, "behold the sacred red road that runs from where we always face to where the giant is (north and south). This road shall be your nation, from this road you shall receive the power to do good." The red road is the good or straight way for the north is purity and the south is the source of life. The red road is similar to the Christian "straight and narrow way'; it is the vertical of the cross. Black Elk tells us that red represents all that is sacred, especially the earth, for we should remember that it is from the earth that our bodies come and it is to her that they return.

In terms of our personal journey, the Red Road represents a choice or direction for us to go. Examination of the previous footprint revealed Maslow's higher levels of need, specifically self-realization, the need for confidence and self-worth. Concentration on our inner self will point the way to who we are and the potential of what we really can become. This final footprint leads us to the most critical step, one that involves an even higher level of need: self-actualization.

Maslow goes into great detail in describing the self-actualizing person. He said that the self-actualizing person enjoys solitude and privacy, particularly as it relates to a sense of security and self-sufficiency. Self-actualizing persons are more aware of their environment, both human and nonhuman. They have a high level of acceptance of self, others and nature. Self-actualizing persons are not ashamed or guilty about their human nature, with its shortcomings, imperfections, frailties, and weaknesses. Nor are they critical of these aspects in other people. They respect and esteem themselves and others. Self-actualizing persons repeatedly experience awe, pleasure, and wonder in their everyday world. In varying degrees, they have feelings of wonder with limitless horizons opening up, followed by a conviction that the experience was important and must carryover into everyday life. They have a deep feeling of empathy, sympathy, and compassion for human beings in general. Most important, this feeling is unconditional. And finally, the self-actualizing person is highly ethical and willing to learn from anyone.

One might say that the Red Road is actually the road to self-actualization. Campbell mentioned the sacred place as being our "bliss station" but in terms of our personal fulfillment, the goal is to journey forward on a path that is waiting for us. The fourth grandfather called the Red Road the path of peace and harmony and so it is. By finding your center and realizing who you are, you are now ready to travel forward and put action into your dream, or as Campbell tells us, follow your bliss.

We are not alone, Campbell continues, for every inch along the way we are helped by "hidden hands." Doors will open, he says, doors that you never knew were there. If you follow your bliss, you'll have that joy and that refreshment you need all the time.

He uses the analogy of an umbilical cord to signify the lifeline aiding us as we travel out from our center and journey along the road we will travel. It is our connection to what is real for us. The world is constantly trying to distract us with occasional concerns, but holding to this umbilical cord helps us to deal with life's everyday issues, a technique one has to work out for one's self. But he promises, sooner or later we'll find the capacity that's waiting to be awakened and will lead us to this other place. It is there you will learn to recognize your own depths, where the deep sense of being informed is felt, a place where your soul and body want to go.

But as with most elements of our lives, the destination is secondary. It is the journey that most involves us. How we travel through our days, as well as the direction we choose to take are really most important.

After the massacre at Wounded Knee, the people were lost. They were looking for a way to go. But this would take time and opportunity. The following Meditative Reading gives Black Elk's account of the days following Wounded Knee and describes his involvement in the fight.

Linda L. Stampoulos

Meditative Reading

Walk the Red Road
The Lesson and Legacy of Black Elk

At that time I could see that the hoop was broken and all scattered out and I thought, "I am going to try my best to get my people back into the hoop again." At that time the wilds were vanishing and it seemed the spirits altogether forgot me and I felt almost like a dead man going around—I was actually dead at this time, that's all. In my vision they had predicted that I was chosen to be intercessor for my people so it was up to me to do my utmost for my people and everything that I did not do for my people, it would be my fault. If I were in poverty my people would also be in poverty, and if I were helpless and died, my people would die also. But it was up to me to scheme a certain way for myself to prosper for the people. If I prosper, my people would also prosper.

This is how I felt and what I really wanted to do is for us to make that tree bloom. On this tree we shall prosper. Therefore my children are relative-like and therefore we shall go back into the hoop and here we'll cooperate and stand as one. That is why I want to go to Harney Peak, because here I will send the voices to my six grandfathers. I saw many happy faces behind those six grandfathers and maybe it will be that my family will be the happy faces. Our families will multiply and prosper after we get this tree to blooming.

And here at the center of the earth I am now at the same place and I see all the good things of the earth that were to be my people's. The four-leggeds and the wings of the air, through them, relative-like we should be, and through them we should send up our voices to you, O Great Spirit! In setting me at the center of the earth and showing me all the good things that were to be my people's and now my people are in despair and I will thus send a voice again. You have set me here and made me behold all things, the good things, and at this very place, the center of the earth, you have promised to set the tree that was to bloom. But I have fallen away this causing the tree never to bloom again; but there may be a root that is still alive and give strength and moisture of your good things that you have given to us people and through all the powers of the four quarters, the mother earth and the four-leggeds of the earth and the wings of the air through whom we should send up our sighs and voices. May you behold them and also behold me and trust me and hear me, O Great Spirit, my Grandfather!

In sending up my voice I prayed that you may set the tree to bloom again so that my people will see many happy days. The six grandfathers, my grandfathers, through your power you have sent me to the center of the earth and showed me all the good things that were to be mine. Hear me, that my people will live, and find a way that my people will prosper. Again, and the last time probably, I will recall my vision and call on you again for help, six grandfathers, representing the Great Spirit and the two-leggeds on earth and the four quarters of the earth and also all the beings of the earth. May I send a voice once again so that you may hear me and bring my people back into the hoop and at the center there should be the tree that was to bloom and help us and have mercy on us. Hear me, O Great Spirit, that my people will get back into the sacred hoop and that the tree may bloom and that my people will live the ways you have set for them, and if they live, they may see the happy days and the happy land that you have promised.

Linda L. Stampoulos

Talking Points

Walk the Red Road
The Lesson and Legacy of Black Elk

Authorities differ on the number of Indians present and killed at Wounded Knee. But according to Major Whitside, to whom they surrendered, he reported them officially as numbering 120 men and 250 women and children. Among those who surrendered were about 70 refugees from the bands of Sitting Bull and Hump. No exact account of the dead could be made immediately after the fight, on account of a second attack by another party of Indians coming up from the agency. (Black Elk was part of this group, and he was wounded during the fight.) The official number was lower than actual according to Mooney since some of the dead and wounded that had been left on the field were undoubtedly carried off by their friends before the Calvary's burial party came out three days later, but received no notice in official reports. Mooney goes on to say that On New Year's day of 1891, three days after the battle, a detachment of troops went out to Wounded Knee to gather up and bury the Indian dead and to bring in the wounded who might be still alive on the field. In the meantime there had been a heavy snowstorm, culminating in a blizzard. The bodies of the slaughtered men, women, and children were found lying under the snow, frozen stiff and covered with blood. Four babies were found alive under the snow, wrapped in the shawls and lying beside their dead mothers, whose last thought had been of them. They were all badly frozen and only one lived. He states that the tenacity of life so characteristic of these Indigenous people was strikingly illustrated in the case of these wounded and helpless Indian women and children who had lived three days through a Dakota blizzard, without food, shelter, or attention to their wounds.

This is a lesson from the tragedy at Wounded Knee, the recognition of the tenacity of life that was "strikingly illustrated" by those who survived. A baby survived four days alone in a blizzard! Nothing we ever face will compare to what the Sioux Indians experienced during their last years of freedom. What power sustained them during the massacre? How were they able to survive a blizzard? Many say this is all part of the Great Mystery, the unknown power that surrounds us. Our quest then is to acknowledge this mystery and seek to discover its power: that burning point that becoming point when you are fearless and desireless, not driven by need or want, but by the energy that comes from within.

We have followed the ancient path illuminated by the beacons shining from the Great Vision. This final footprint leads us to the edge. Black Elk prayed that his people may once more go back into the sacred hoop, find the good red road, and nourish the sacred tree. The Red Road stretches before us. We have the guideposts, the footprints that have risen from the bloody snow. It is time to accept the personal challenge and begin our quest toward self realization and the eventual self actualization that will be ours.

Hanble Wakan

The Great Vision

Epilogue: The Great Vision

As promised, the author presents the following complete narrative of the Great Vision given to Black Elk. As a note to the reader: the narrative is told by Black Elk as he traveled through the realms of spiritual imagery that were common to his culture and as he understood their unique importance.

Joseph Campbell explains that as a boy, Black Elk had a psychological experience. He experienced a transformation of consciousness, one that brought him from his own personal unconscious to the edge of the collective unconscious. For the young boy, it was overwhelming but true to the shamanic experience. He was shown the prophetic future of his tribe, both in positive and negative terms. The negative, as we know, was the terrible defeat and radical change of their way of life; while on the positive side, he saw his nation's hoop and realized that it was one of many hoops, and there was cooperation of all the hoops of all the nations in grand procession.

"I saw myself on the central mountain of the world, the highest place, and through the vision, I was seeing the world in a sacred manner. The central mountain was Harney Peak, South Dakota, but I realized the central mountain is everywhere."

Campbell tells us that in mythological terms, the center of the world is the hub of the universe. The central point of the world is a point where stillness and movement are together; movement is time and stillness is eternity. Realizing the relationship between the temporal and the eternal is key to the meaning of life. To realize that this moment in your life is actually a moment of eternity is the mythological experience. It is a concept not easy to grasp but critical in trying to come to grips with the vision today: that is to relate the eternal aspects of what you are doing in the temporal consciousness, the here and now.

"So," Campbell asks, "is the sacred mountain Harney Peak? Jerusalem? Rome? Mexico City?" "No," Campbell continues, "these are geographic places that connote the center of the world. They are symbolic of the spiritual principle of the center of the world."

What Black Elk was telling us, Campbell says, is that the shining point where all lines intersect lies in everyone, and each of us is a manifestation of that mystery.

The Great Vision

When I was nine years old, many Pawnees got killed and the camp was now going toward the Rocky Mountains. I was now able to shoot a prairie chicken, a grouse, and other things quite well. I was also training in slinging the mud at this time.

Close to the Crow Camp on the Little Bighorn I was riding along and I heard something calling me again. Just before we got to Greasy Grass Creek (the Little Bighorn), they camped again for the night. There was a man by the name of Man Hip who invited me for supper. While eating I heard a voice. I heard someone say, "It is time, now they are calling you." I knew then that I was called upon by the spirits so I thought I'd just go where they wanted me to. As I came out of the tent both of my thighs hurt me.

The next morning they broke camp and I started out with some others on horseback. We stopped at a creek to get a drink. When I got off my horse I crumbled down and I couldn't walk. The boys helped me up and when the people camped again, I was very sick. They went on, taking me to the Sioux band camp and I was still pretty sick. Both my legs and arms were swollen badly and even my face. This all came suddenly.

As I lay in the tipi I could see through the tipi the same two men whom I saw before and they were coming from the clouds, then I recognized them as the same men I had seen before in my first vision. They came and stood off aways from me and stopped, saying: "Hurry up, your grandfather is calling you." When they started back I got up and started to follow them. Just as I got out of the tipi I could see the two men going back into the clouds and there was a small cloud coming down toward me at the same time, which stood before me. I got on top of the cloud and was raised up, following the two men, and when I looked back, I saw my father and mother looking at me. When I looked back I felt sorry that I was leaving them.

I followed those men on up into the clouds and they showed me a vision of a bay horse standing there in the middle of the clouds. One of the men said "Behold him, the horse who has four legs, you shall see." I stood there and looked at the horse and it began to speak. It said: "Behold me; my life history you shall see. Furthermore, behold them, those where the sun goes down, their lives' history you shall see."

I looked over there and saw twelve black horses toward the west, where the sun goes down. All the horses had on their necks necklaces of buffalo hoofs. I saw above the twelve head of horses birds. I was very scared of those twelve head of horses because I could see the lightning and thunder around them.

Then they showed me the twelve white horses with necklaces of elks' teeth and said: "Behold them, those who are where the giant lives (the north). Then I saw some white geese flying around over the horses.

Then I turned around toward the east, the sun shines continually. The men said: "Behold them, those where the sun shines continually." I saw twelve head of horses, all sorrels and those sorrels had horns and there were some eagles flying above the sorrels.

Then I turned to the place where you always face, the south, and saw twelve head of buckskin horses. They said: "Behold him, those where you always face." These horses had horns.

At the beginning of the vision they were all horses, only two sets had necklaces, the blacks and the whites, and two had horns: the sorrels and the buckskins.

When I had seen it all, the bay horse said to me: "Your grandfathers are having a council, these shall take you; so take courage." Then these horses went into formation of twelve abreast in four lines—blacks, whites, sorrels, buckskins. As they stood, the bay horse looked to the west and neighed. I looked over there and saw great clouds of horses in all colors and they all neighed back to this horse and it sounded like thunder. Then the horse neighed to the north and the horses came through there and neighed back again. These horses were in all colors also. Then the bay horse looked to the east and he neighed and some more horses neighed back. The bay horse looked southward and neighed and the horses neighed back to him from there.

The bay horse said to me: "Behold them, your horses are dancing." I looked around and saw millions of horses circling around me—a sky full of horses. Then the bay horse said: "Make haste." The horse began to go beside me and the forty-eight horses followed us. I looked around and all the horses that were running changed into buffalo, elk, and all kinds of animals and fowls and they all went back to the four quarters.

The Bay Horse leads Black Elk to the Cloud Tipi of the Six Grandfathers

I followed the bay horse and it took me to a place on a cloud under a rainbow gate and there were sitting my six grandfathers, sitting inside of a rainbow door, and the horses stopped behind me. I saw on either side of me a man whom I recognized as those of the first vision. The horses took their original positions at the four quarters.

One of the grandfathers said to me: "Do not fear, come right in" (through the rainbow door). So I went in and stood before them. The horses in the four quarters all neighed to cheer me as I entered the rainbow door.

The grandfather representing where the sun goes down said: "Your grandfathers all over the world and the earth are having a council and there you were called, so here you are. Behold then, those where the sun goes down; from thence they shall come, you shall see. From them you shall know the willpower of myself, for they shall take you to the center of the earth, and the nations of all kinds shall tremble. Behold where the sun continually shines, for they shall take you there."

The first grandfather then showed me a wooden cup with water, turning it toward me. He said: "Take courage and be not afraid, for you will know him. And furthermore, behold him, whom you shall represent. By representing him, you shall be very powerful on earth in medicines and all powers. He is your spirit and you are his body and his name is Eagle Wing Stretches."

When I looked up I saw flames going up from the rainbow. The first grandfather gave me a cup of water and also a bow and arrow and said: "Behold them, what I give you shall depend on, for you shall go against our enemies and you shall be a great warrior." Then he gave me that cup of water and said: "Behold, take this, and with this you shall be great." (This means that I should kill all sickness on earth with this water.)

After this he got up and started to run toward where the sun goes down and as he ran he changed into a black horse as he faced me. The five men left said: "Behold him." And this black horse changed into a poor horse.

The second grandfather rose and said to me: "Take this and make haste." So I took an herb out of the second grandfather's hand. And as I turned toward the dying horse, I held it toward the black horse and this holy herb cured the black horse making him strong and fat once again.

The second grandfather represented the north. He said: "Behold the mother earth, for you shall create a nation." (This means that I am going to cure lots of sickness with this herb—bring children back to life.) The bay horse stood with the black horse and said to me: "Father, paint me, for I shall make a nation on the earth." The second grandfather of the north said again: "Take courage and behold, for you shall represent the wing of the great giant that lives." The second grandfather stood up and ran to the north and as he turned around he changed himself again into a white goose. I looked to where the black horses were and they were thunders and the northern white horses turned into white geese. The second grandfather said: "Behold then, your grandfather, for they shall fly in circles from one end of the earth to the other. Through this power of the north I will make everybody cry as geese do when they go north in the spring because the hardship is over.

First grandfather's song:

> *They are appearing, may you behold.*
> *They are appearing, may you behold.*
> *The thunder nation is appearing, may you behold.*

Second grandfather's song:

> *They are appearing, may you behold.*
> *They are appearing, may you behold.*
> *The white geese nation is appearing, may you behold.*

The third grandfather, where the sun continually shines, says: "Younger brother, take courage, for across the earth they shall take you. Behold them." (pointing to the morning star and below the star there were two men flying), "from them you shall have power. All the fowls of the universe, these he has wakened and also he has wakened the beings on the earth" (animals, people, etc.) As the third grandfather said this, he held in his hand a peace pipe, which had a spotted eagle outstretched on the handle of the pipe; apparently the eagle was alive for it was moving. He said: "Behold him." Then the red man lay down and changed into a buffalo before he got up. When he was standing up, the third grandfather said "Behold him" again. The buffalo ran back to the east and when he looked at the horses in this direction they all turned into buffalo.

The fourth grandfather said to me: "Younger brother, behold me; a nation's center of the earth I shall give you with the power of the four quarters. With the power of the four quarters like relatives you shall walk. Behold the four quarters." And after he said this I looked and saw that at each of the four quarters there was a chief. At the time I grew up into manhood there was no war and the Indians all became white men and if there had been the right feeling among the Indians I would have been the greatest, most powerful medicine man of the ages.

The fourth grandfather had a stick in his hand and he said: "Behold this, with this to the nation's center of the earth many you shall save." I looked at the stick and saw that it was sprouting out and at the top there were all kinds of birds singing. The fourth grandfather said: "With this you shall brace yourself as a cane and thus your nation shall brace themselves with this as a cane and upon this cane you shall make a nation. Behold the earth, for across it there are two roads. Behold the sacred road from where the giant is to where we always face. Behold, this road shall be your nation. From this road you shall receive good." (Meaning red sacred road from north to south, a good road for good spirits)

Next the fourth grandfather pointed to the road from where the sun shines continually to where the sun goes down and said: "Behold the black road, for it is the road to the Thunder-beings" (road of fearfulness); or, "Behold the black road for it shall be a fearful road. With this road you shall defend yourself." Whenever I go to war I shall get powers to destroy any enemies. From the red road I get power and do good. From east to west I have power to destroy and from north to south power to do good.

"Behold the earth with four ascents you shall walk." (This power will be with me for four generations.) The fourth grandfather turned around and started to the south and then he rolled on the ground and became a horse and he rolled on the ground once more and became an elk. He then stood among the buckskins and they too turned into elks.

The fifth grandfather represented the Great Spirit above. He said: "Boy, I sent for you and you came. Behold me, my power you shall see." He stretched his hands out and turned into a spotted eagle. Then he said: "Behold them; they, the fowls of the universe, shall come to you. Things in the skies shall be like relatives" (meaning stars). "They shall take you across the earth with my power. Your grandfathers shall attack an enemy and be unable to destroy him, but you will have the power to destroy. You shall go with courage. This is all." Then the eagle flew up over my head and I saw the animals and birds all coming toward me to perform a duty.

Then the sixth grandfather said: "Boy, take courage, you wanted my power on earth, so you shall know me. You shall have my power in going back to the earth. Your nation on earth shall have great difficulties. There you shall go. Behold me, for I will depart. (The sixth grandfather was a very old man with very white hair.) I saw him go out the rainbow gate. I followed him out the rainbow gate. I was on the bay horse now that had talked to me at the first. I stopped and took a good look at the sixth grandfather and it seemed that I recognized him. I stood there for a while very scared and then as I looked at him longer I knew it was myself as a young man. At the first he was an old man, but he got younger and younger until he was a little boy nine years old. This old man had in his hand a spear.

Black Elk walk the Black Sacred Road from west to east and vanquishes the spirit in the water

I remembered that the grandfather of the west had given me a wooden cup of water and a bow and arrow and with this bow and arrow I was going to destroy the enemy with the power of the fearful road. With the wooden cup of water I was to save mankind. This water was clear and with it I was to raise a nation (like medicine).

My horse turned around and faced the west and all the black horses went and stood behind me in four ranks, twelve abreast—blacks, whites, sorrels, buckskins. They turned around toward the north. "Behold your wind from the north; this wind and an herb they have given you. With this herb and the wind you shall go back to the earth." (With the herb I was to have power to save horses and the wind was included. Whenever I would own a horse, it would be able to run for weeks and weeks without getting out of wind.) We swung around to the east in formation. The grandfather of the east let the pipe go which he was holding and it flew to me: "Behold it, for with this you shall be peaceful with the nations. Behold it, for you shall possess this for the nations on earth." I took the pipe . The eastern grandfather said again: "Behold him who shall appear; from him you shall have power." The morning star was coming up in the east as I looked this way. As I faced them, I noticed that the sorrels of the east had stars on their foreheads and they were very bright. Then we faced the south and the eastern grandfather said: "Behold your black sacred road you shall walk." As I turned around the buckskins lined up into formation and turned around facing the east to take me down the road of destruction. "As you shall walk your nation, the beings all over the universe shall fear you."

They began to go toward the east. They were all following me. I was the leader. I could see ahead of me a lot of birds in the air and behind me they were all fearful of me. There were twelve riders—all right-handed except one and he was called Left Hand Charger. The rider of the white horse was called One Horn Red and they gave me the name Eagle That Stretches Its Wing.

Going east from the highest peak in the west—Pike's Peak, as we went along I noticed that everything on the earth was trembling with fear. I looked back and saw my twelve horseback riders and the horses' manes and tails were decorated with hail and the men had hail all over them. I was riding along as the chief of all the heavens and I looked down and saw the hail falling from these men and horses. I could see the country as I went and I remember well seeing the forks of the Missouri River a man standing amid a flame with the dust around him in the air. I knew then that this was the enemy which was going to attack me. I could see all kinds of creatures dying beneath me, as he had destroyed everything.

As we neared this place we sang a sacred song concerning the peace pipe and the eagle, and all the riders had this for a weapon. The sorrels sang first. The song that represents the four quarters:

I, myself, have sent them a-fleeing
Because I wore the feather of an eagle.
I, myself sent them a-fleeing.

*I, myself, have sent them a-fleeing.
For I wore the relic of the wind.
I, myself, have sent them a-fleeing.*

The Thunder-beings sang then:

*I, myself, send them a-fleeing.
For I wore the relic of the hail.
I, myself, send them a-fleeing.*

Then the ones on the west sang:

*I, myself, send them a-fleeing
I, myself, send then a-fleeing.*

Then the water splashed up as a result of something scared of me, and the flames came rolling out of this same place. The twelve riders from the west attacked this man but could not destroy him. He attacked them and forced them back toward the south. The white riders from the north attacked him but failed also to kill him. The eastern riders attacked him and also failed as he drove them back. They stood facing north. The buckskins from the south also attacked him and failed. After they all had attacked this man and failed, I looked at the splashing water and saw a man painted blue coming out. Then they all hollered: "He is coming!" and ran. They said: "Eagle Wing Stretches, make haste, for your nation all over the universe is in fear, make haste." I could hear, at this time, everything in the universe cheering for me. At this time my bow and arrow changed into a big spear. With the spear and the cup of water in the other hand, I immediately charged on the enemy myself. As I attacked, everybody cheered for me, telling me to "Make haste!" Just as the man got to the water, I swooped down on him and stabbed him through the heart. You could see the lightning from my spear as I stabbed him. I took him and threw him quite a distance. Just as I took the spear out, the man turned into a turtle. After I had killed the enemy the horse troops came by and hit (couped) the enemy and then they went back. Everything that had been dead came back to life and cheered me for killing that enemy. (This means that sometime in the future I am going to kill an enemy in some future battle.)

Black Elk walks the Red Sacred Road from south to north

I was taken to the four parts of the earth. I now came down to the earth and we traveled along the Missouri River. Soon we saw a camp in a circle. One of them pointed to the camp and said: "Behold that nation; yours it is." They stopped on the south side and gave me the stick with the branches on it. They said: "Behold this stick; with this stick you shall walk with your nation where the big giant lives (north)." I was to give this stick to my people so that they will depend on it and with it they shall walk the red road and also with the pipe. They showed me the people that I was going to raise. The southern spirit said: "Behold them, your nation and your people, make haste."

Before me they showed me a tipi of the village, which was on the east side by itself. Here I could see women, children and men dying. The southern spirit said: "Behold them and make haste." I saw a man whose body was turning gray and whose mouth had red flames coming out of it. I was very much frightened at the sight and tried to get away. As I went down there, the wind was blowing from the south to the north now. I passed in front of the tipi and all the people got up. The southern spirit said: "That's the way you shall save men." I was to be a sacred man when I got back to earth (a wakan wicasa, holy man).

Then they took me back to the middle of the camp where the people gathered all around me. The southern spirit then said to me: "Give your nation the sacred pipe and also your sacred flowering stick." I presented the pipe and the stick to the people and they all rejoiced. They were going to depend on that stick for peace and health. The southern spirit said: "Your nation shall walk that red road" (from south to north) "toward where the giant lives." The northern grandfather then said: "Give your sacred herb to your people; also give them your sacred wind so they shall face the wind with courage. Also they shall walk as a relative of your wind. Behold your people for they shall break camp and go forth. Behold them." (Breaking camp here means that they shall be prosperous always.)

These men were going to pray to the spirits and call upon them. They were ready to pray for the spirits. One among the people hollered out: "Hey, hey, hey, hey!" One of the grandfathers said to the people then: "Behold your grandfathers, for they shall walk forth with you." The people broke camp and one of each of the horses went forward. The black horse rider took the herb with him; the white horse rider took the sacred wind with him; the sorrel rider took the sacred pipe; the buckskin rider took the flowering stick. All of the people were going along. Four more riders, one from each quarter, came forth and presented me with a hoop, and with that hoop I was to make a nation and under that we were to prosper.

The circle represented the old people that represented the nation. The center of it represented the prosperity of the nation. I was to raise a nation either in prosperity or in difficulty. In presenting the sacred hoop to me (each is a nation), the spirit from the west said: "Behold this sacred hoop; it is the people you shall have" (meaning that I would own these people). In his left hand the spirit held the hoop and in his right hand he held the bow and arrow. He said: "You shall have this nation and with this bow and arrow on earth your worst enemy you shall conquer." At the same time he held this wooded cup of water, and he said: "With this the wildest enemies will be tame." (I could capture anything without being hurt. With that bow and arrow my people should be able to do the same things as I can. They used that on Custer and there wasn't one of them who did not have an arrow in his skin. This worked in the Custer fight very well.)

The Thunder-beings (lightning) have the power to kill and the water the power to heal. We could depend on the water to live on and the lightning to kill with. From this water all the herbs grow. Water is the great power. The water in the wooded cup represented a big lake. When I was conquering the spirit at the head of the Missouri River I was getting power from the water, and now I get power from the water the same as then. Everything is dependent on water. If I had not conquered the bad spirit, I would not have had the power. I had conquered the power of the water in conquering this bad spirit. The three forks of the Missouri River is the source of the Great Water. When I had conquered the bad spirit I had gained control over the power of the water. At this place there had been many people who had died without water and I came and destroyed the enemy and the people were then all living well again. I was killing draught and also I could bring my people out of any difficulty that they might have.

Any man who sees the morning star will see something more, meaning that he will be worth something, and if he does not see the morning star, he is not worth anything ever.

I think about this dream often. It is in me. And many times

I feel bad about it and other times I feel good about it. It was a power dream and it will never be forgotten until I die. You take a bunch of honey bees. You know that it always has a king of the hive in it. All the bees obey the king and he wants to get along with all the bees. My vision is something like that. I am liked by all people and I can influence them. Everybody has respect for me—even the white people. The moment I see anybody I want to get along with him and I always do get along with him.

The southern spirit said furthermore to me: "with the power of the four quarters shall return to their places on the four quarters." The spirit of the west said: "Behold the man who sits where the sun goes down; with his power also the greenward day." Rain comes mostly from the west here. (West represents spring and summer.) The southern spirit said: "Behold him where the giant lives for you shall have his power also—a white day, representing winter. They all returned to their four quarters now. The southern spirit said: "Behold him where the sun shines continually, for you shall have his power. Behold him where you always face, for you shall have his power and also the yellow day," Yellow day represented autumn and furthermore the night. The nighttime is the best time to think with the stars out. The southern spirit said: "Behold your morning star, for your nation shall have a knowledge from that morning star. Now the people shall walk with their power, the power they have received."

In my nation they made four chiefs and four advisors. The people were in formation for moving farther, walking thus:

First, the four spirit horsemen leading the people.
Second, the four chiefs leading the people.
Third, the four advisors leading the people.
Fourth, the old men with canes.

Fifth, the old women with canes.
Sixth, myself following them in the rear.

The southern spirit said again to me: "Behold the four old men; present thy sacred hoop to them, for they are really grandfathers and great grandfathers way back which the tribe came from." They were in order, the younger generations and then the older generations following. They are marching. The southern spirit said: "Thus I will walk in the rear; sending a voice out, I thus walk." I was leading my people so that they will all be prosperous. As I walk I am going to pray to the Great Spirit.

I wore an ornament of the sacred hoop.
This nation shall send a voice for their children.
(Means these people will prosper and increase.)

Song about the people increasing. Words sung by the southern spirit:

A voice I am sending as I walk (twice)
A sacred hoop I wore.
Thus, a voice I send as I walk (twice)
(To future generations.)

The first child they called for was the name of Spotted Deer Woman, calling unborn children. The next one I called for was Young Buffalo Woman. The people are on a good road now and walking toward where the child lives. These people show go up four more generations. "Behold your nation as they walk and to the first ascent and show them another such and so-on. When the get to the first generation (ascent) all the creatures on the earth and in the air shall rejoice because the first ascent represents the people here on earth and they are going to multiply and increase and at the same time prosper. One of the old men said, showing me the sacred hoop: "Behold a good nation, a sacred nation, again they will walk toward good land, the land of plenty, and no suffering shall there be. A nation you shall create and it shall be a sacred nation" meaning that I was given the power to raise a nation.

Song in the first ascent:

May you behold this I have asked to be made over. (twice)
A good nation I have asked to be made over.
May you behold this I have asked to be made over. (twice)
A sacred nation I have asked to be made over.
May you behold this I have asked to be made over. (twice)

After singing this song, the people went on. When they got to the end, the men and women began sending voices for their children and again they stopped at the end of the second generation.

The man of the south says: "Behold, you shall prevent the making of the clouds." They were now at the second ascent and I was given the power to defend my people at all dangerous times and to keep them from destruction. The south man says: "Behold your nation they have given you, for they shall be like unto the animals and the fowls; thus they shall walk." As they started, the men and women were sending voices for their children again. At this moment the whole people walking on the good road transformed into buffalo and elk and even fowls of the air and were traveling on the good road toward the north. (Meaning that the Indian generations have dreams and are like unto the animals of this world. Some have visions about elks, birds, and even gophers or eagles.

People will be like the animals—take the animals' virtues and strength.)

As the beasts walk along I saw the Indians from thence on would be like unto animals and will have rules of their own. As I noticed this, all the animals became restless and were all in fear and were afraid that they weren't what they were. This nation was walking in a sacred manner. Just before the people stopped I could hear them calling for their chiefs. They were sacred and wanted the chiefs to come at once. After sending voices for their chiefs they stopped. The southern spirit said: "Behold your nation walking in a sacred manner; from thence they shall walk in difficulty. Now you shall go forth to the center of the nation's hoop. Behold this, for you shall go forth to the center of the nation's hoop; with this you shall have power."

(The third ascent represented all kinds of animals and fowls, and from there on every man has his own vision and rules. The fourth ascent will be terrible.)

They (the white men) couldn't get along with us and they did not look after us. The birds and other animals are the only race that we really get along with. We, the Indian race, and the beings on this earth—the buffalo, elk, and the birds in the air—they are just like relatives to us and we get along fine with them, for we get our power from them and from them we live. The white people came on this continent and put us Indians in a fence and they put another fence somewhere else and put our game into it. When the buffalo and elk were all gone, the Great Spirit will look upon the whites for this and perhaps something will happen.

"Behold when you shall go forth to the center of the nation's hoop you shall run into the four quarters." (Nobody shall be sacred before me. Wherever I go, in front of me there will be no hard task for me. Every task I undertake I will push through. It won't be hard for me either.)

Then the spirit sang a powerful song:

The four quarters may you run to.
(Meaning that I will get power from them.)
No man will be sacred before you.
They have said to me.

At this time, everything that was given to me by the spirits I had. The man of the south said again to me: "Behold your grandfathers who have given you the sacred relics. Whenever you shall look upon an enemy, it shall tremble" (meaning that I shall conquer any kind of opposition). "Remember this" (meaning the cup of water I got), "for from this the people shall have strength and power."

As they stood ready to go on that fourth ascent of the earth, the south spirit said: "Look upon your nation." The beasts transformed themselves into humans and they were all very poor. ("Oh, gee! It was a sight," says Black Elk.) There were lots of sick children—all pale and it looked like a dying nation. They showed me a circle village and all the people were very poor in there. All the horses were hide and bones and here and there you could hear the wail of women and also men. Some of them were dying and some were dead. Quite an epidemic there. Again the southern spirit said: "Behold your nation." (Meaning they were going to show me something terrible. I am now ready to return to the earth after being in the air with the fowls. The three ascents were all spiritual, but now I am to see the fourth quarter and in this they were showing me all the difficulties.)

Black Elk receives the Healing Herb of the North and the Sacred Tree is established at the center of the nation's hoop

As I looked down upon the people, there stood on the north side a man painted red all over his body and he had with him a lance (Indian spear) and he walked into the center of the sacred nation's hoop and lay down and rolled himself on the ground and when he got up he was a buffalo standing right in the center of the nation's hoop. The buffalo rolled and when he got up there was an herb there in his place. The herb plant grew up and bloomed so that I could see what it looked like---what kind of an herb it was from the bloom. After the buffalo's arrival the people looked better and then when the buffalo turned into an herb, the people all got up and seemed to be well. Even the horses got up and stretched themselves and neighed. Then a little breeze came from the north and I could see that the wind was in the form of a spirit and as it went over the people all the dead things came to life. All the horses pulled up their tails and neighed and began to prance around.

The southern spirit said: "Behold you have seen the powers of the north in the forms of man, buffalo, herb and wind, The people shall follow the man's steps; like him they shall walk and like the buffalo they shall live and with the herb they shall have knowledge. They shall be like relatives to the wind." (From the man in the illustration they should be healthy, from the buffalo they shall get meat, from the herb they shall get knowledge of diseases. The north wind will give them strong endurance.)

The southern spirit speaks again: "Behold him they have sent forth to the center of the nation's hoop." Then I saw the pipe with the spotted eagle flying to the center of the nation's hoop. The morning star went along with the pipe. They flew from the east to the center. "With this your nation's offering as they walk. They will be like unto him. With the pipe they shall have peace in everything. Behold your eagle, for your nation like relatives they shall be. Behold the morning star, relative-like they shall be, from whence they shall have wisdom." Just then the morning star appeared and all the people looked up to it and the horses neighed and the dogs barked.

(The flowering stick was in the middle of the nation's hoop again.)

The southern spirit said: "Behold the circle of the sacred hoop, for the people shall be like unto it; and if they are like unto this, they shall have power, because there is no end to this hoop and in the center of this hoop they shall raise their children." The sacred hoop means the continents of the world and the people shall stand as one. Everything reproduces here inside the hoop.

They put the sacred stick into the center of the hoop and you could hear birds singing all kinds of songs by this flowering stick and the people and animals all rejoiced and hollered. The women were sending up their tremolos. The men said: "Behold it; from there we shall multiply, for it is the greatest of the greatest sticks." This stick will take care of the people and at the same time it will multiply. We live under it like chickens under the wing. We live under the flowering stick like under the wing of a hen.

Depending on the sacred stick we shall walk and it will be with us always. From this we will raise our children and under the flowering stick we will communicate with our relatives—beast and bird—as one people. This is the center of the life of the nation.

The sacred stick is the cottonwood tree (rustling tree, can wakan). The nation represents this tree, and if they grow up they will multiply like the birds, etc. This tree never had a chance to bloom because the white men came. The trunk is the chief of the people. If this tree had seen a bloom probably I or one of my descendants would be great chiefs.

The people camped there. I was on the bay horse again on the west side and was with another man. This man is still living today and probably I could have made him a medicine man, but I never did it as yet, because I have never seen him. This man lives at Grass Creek and he knows nothing about this, nevertheless. This man's name was One Side. One Side had a bow and arrow in one hand and a cup of water in the other. I saw that the people were getting ready for a storm and they were fixing their tipis to make them stronger for the storm. The storm cloud was approaching and swallows were coming under the cloud and I, myself, and One Side were coming on top of the cloud. (We were traveling on the fourth ascent and I saw people from the third ascent on the fourth ascent.)

It was raining on earth now. A spirit said to me that they had shown me everything there was to do on earth and that I was to do it myself now. He sang this song and it went like this:

> *A good nation I will make over.*
> *The nation above has said this to me.*
> *They have given me the power to make over this nation.*

The cloud then swept over the village and the people stood in the west. When they turned around, the cloud was all gone. The cloud christened them with water. They all hollered: "Eagle Wing Stretches, A-ha-hey!" (meaning "Thanks to Eagle Wing Stretches!"). The people on earth started on the good road again, the red road, and I was forced to give all my relics to the people with the exception of the bow and arrow. The horses were all very fat now, so the people began to break camp. The people accepted what I gave them and I went ahead on the good road. (The bow and arrow represent lightning.)

Black Elk kills the dog in the flames and receives the Healing Herb of the West

The western spirit said (people turning toward the west): "Behold where the sun goes down, you shall walk. Everything that lacks strength you shall make over as you walk." I was on the bay horse and One Side on a bay also; we led the blacks, whites, sorrels, and buckskins westward. As they went into formation one of the black horse riders, Left Hand Charger, said: "Behold your grandfathers; they will seek your enemy. Take courage, you shall be the leader." Just as he said this he called for someone by the name of Brave Thunder and they all hollered for Black Elk, Eagle Wing Stretches.

Soon I could see a flame coming up from the earth. They went around it and Left Hand Charger went around the left side instead of right and we followed. (They were on the west side of the flame when they stopped.) When we got around it, it was a sight. You could hear the crashing of the thunder and lightning. Left Hand Charger was ready to charge and he saw the flame of it. The horse's tail was lightning and the flames were coming out of his horse's nose. As I went I could see nothing but I could only hear the thunder and lightning and of course I could see the flames. All the rest of the troops went around the enemy   Left Hand Charger made a vain attempt to kill the enemy. A spirit said, "Eagle Wing Stretches, take courage; your turn has come."

We got ready and started down on the cloud on our bay horses. One Side and I were coming down together. I could see the lightning coming off my arrows as I descended. Just as we were about to hit the earth, we struck something. I could hear thunder rolling and everyone cheered for me saying, "Unhee!" ("Kill!") I could hear my people on the good road saying,

"Who killed that enemy?" I heard someone say then that Eagle Wing Stretches has done it and they all cheered again, "Un hah hey!" I made a swoop again on the west side of the enemy, whatever it was, and when I killed it, I looked at it and it was a dog which had a very funny color. One side of him was white and the other side was black. Each one of them struck the dog (couped), meaning they all had a hand in killing it.

The western spirit said: "We are now going to show you a flipping. Behold him, for you shall make him over." They showed me a b lack horse that was brown-like and he was very poor, like skin and bones. Then the west spirit presented me with an herb and said: "Take this and go forth in haste," I took the herb and made a circle over the horse and as I did this they all said: "A hey, a hey!" (calling for spirit power). After I had made the circle over the horse, the horse neighed and began to roll, It was a beautiful shiny stallion. His mane was streaming in the form of a cloud all around him and he had dapples all over him. Every time he snorted there was a flash of lightning and his eyes were as bright as stars. Then the stallion went forth and stopped suddenly, facing the west. He neighed and you could see the dust flying over there as he neighed. In this dust there were a million horses coming. These horses were happy and full of pep. This stallion dashed toward the north and stopped and neighed. Then you could see millions of horses coming out of the dust from this stallion neighing dust in front of him. The stallion then dashed at the east and faced it and neighed and saw some more horses and then he did the same thing toward the south.

Then the black spirit (western grandfather) said: "Behold them for these are your horses. Your horses shall come neighing to you. Your horses shall dance and you shall see. Behold them; all over the universe you have finished." Then there appeared before him four beautiful virgins standing there dressed in red. One of the virgins held the sacred pipe. "Behold your virgins all over the universe; through them the earth shall be happy. From all over the universe they are coming to see them."

The black spirit sang a song (the horse dance):

My horses prancing they are coming from all over the universe.
My horses neighing they are coming, prancing they are coming.
All over the universe my horses are coming.

The dappled black stallion sang this song now:

They will dance, may you behold them. (four times)
A horse nation will dance, may you behold them. (four times)

The horse's voice went all over the universe like a radio and everyone heard it. It was more beautiful than anything could be. All the fowls, beasts, and every living thing heard this horse sing. The birds, horses, tree leaves, and everything in the universe danced to the music of the horse's song. It was so beautiful that they just couldn't help dancing.

After singing, the black stallion spoke saying: "All over the universe everything is finished and your nation of nations is rejoicing." Meaning that everything is living—trees, flowers, grass, and every animal is living now. In the vision I was representing the earth and everything was giving me power. I was given power so that all creatures on earth would be happy.

At the end of the fourth ascent I could see the horses all going back to their homes. The black stallion started back to the west where his home was. The birds and everything sang and the women sang and the tree leaves sang as they went to the four quarters.

The black horse rider from the west speaks: "All over the universe they have finished a day of happiness." As he said this the day was very beautiful, the day was green, the birds were singing, the creeks were singing as they flowed clearly along. You could see the people down there very happy. The deer and the buffalo were leaping and running. The country was all very beautiful—fruit was growing up in great abundance.

Black Elk is taken to the center of the Earth and receives the Daybreak Star Herb

The western black spirit said: "Behold this day, for this day is yours." I will have the power to shed many happy days on people, they tell me. "Take courage, for we shall take you to the center of the earth. They [the spirits] said: "Behold the center of the earth for we are taking you there." As I looked I could see great mountains with rocks and forests on them. I could see all colors of light flashing out of the mountains to the four quarters. Then they took me on top of a high mountain where I could see all over the earth. Then they told me to take courage for they were taking me to the center of the earth. All the sixteen riders of the four quarters were with me going to the center of the earth and also this man by the name of One Side.

We were facing the east and I noticed something queer and found out that it was two men coming from the east and they had wings. On each one's breast was a bright star. The two men came and stood right in front of us and the west black spirit said: "Behold them, for you shall depend upon them." Then as we stood there the daybreak star stood between the two men from the east. There was a little star beside the daybreak star also. They had an herb in their hands and they gave it to me, saying: "Behold this; with this on earth you shall undertake anything and accomplish it." As they presented the herb to me they told me to drop it on earth and when it hit the earth it took root and grew and flowered. You could see a ray of light coming up from the flower, reaching the heavens, and all the creatures of the universe saw this light. (Herbs used by Black Elk are in four colors—yellow, blue, red, white flowers all on one bush. The four-colored flowers represent the four quarters of the earth. This herb is called daybreak star herb,)

The western black spirit said: "Behold all over the universe." As I looked around I could see the country full of sickness and in need of help. This was the future and I was going to cure these people. On the east and north people were rejoicing, and on the south and west they were sick and there was a cloud over them. They said: "Behold them who need help. You shall make them over in the future." After a while I noticed the cloud over the people was a white one and it was probably the white people coming.

The western black spirit sang:

Here and there may you behold. (twice)
All may you behold.
Here and there may you behold. (twice)

They had taken me all over the world and showed me all the powers. They took me to the center of the earth and to the top of the peak they took me to review it all. This last song means that I have already seen it. I was to see the bad and the good. I was to see what is good for humans and what is not good for humans.

Black Elk receives the
Soldier Weed of Destruction

The black horse rider says: "Now your grandfathers, toward them may you walk." (meaning they are going back to the six grandfathers under the flaming rainbow). "You shall now walk toward your grandfathers, but before you there is a man with power. You shall see. Behold him!" I looked down upon the earth and saw a flame which looked to be a man and I couldn't make it out quite. I heard all around voices of moaning and woe. It was sad on earth I felt uneasy and I trembled. We went to the north side of the flaming man. I saw that the flame really was a man now. They showed me the bad in the form of this man who was all in black and had lightning flashes going all over his body. He had horns, all around, the animals and everything were dying and they were all crying. (The black men represented war in general.)

They said: "Behold him. Some day you shall depend upon him. There will be dispute all over the universe." As they said this the man transformed into a gopher and it stood up on its hind legs and turned around. Then this gopher is transformed into an herb. This was the most powerful herb of all that I had gotten. It could be used in war and could destroy a nation. (This was used in war and it was very destructive. If you touch this herb it will kill you at once. Nothing grows anywhere near it because it is killed immediately if it does.)

"Behold him. There will be dispute of nations and you will defend your people with this herb." (I was not old enough when I was supposed to use this herb or else I could have used it and killed many enemies. It was too terrible to use and I was glad that I didn't get to use it. This herb is in the Black Hills. Every animal that nears it dies. Around where it grows there are many skeletons always. This medicine belongs only to me—no one else knows what this herb looks like. It looks like a little tree with crinkly leaves, reddish in color. I call this herb a soldier weed.)

Four riders came up—bay, gray, sorrel, white. The bay rider had a buffalo bonnet on and the latter bonnet was alive. You could see its eyes and nostrils flaming. The horns were long and curled and there were animals of all kinds standing on the horns. The gray rider had on a war bonnet which had many curved horns to the earth. There were only eagles on these horns. The white rider had on a spotted eagle for a bonnet and he had a lance also. The sorrel rider had a lance in his hand and it was a serpent. He had an eagle bonnet. These riders were on the left side of the soldier medicine. Then the four riders sang this song:

My grandfathers, they have caused me to be sacred.
They have caused me to be sacred.
May you behold me.
May you behold me.

As they finished the song, the four riders turned around and made a charge. There was so much smoke that I could not see the riders. I heard rapid gunfire and women and children wailing and the horses screaming in fear, dogs yelping. I heard them hollering for victory.

(I am glad that I did not perform this killing, for I would have not only killed the enemy, but I would probably have killed the women and children of the enemy, but I am satisfied that I have not been well off. Perhaps I would have been a chief if I had obeyed this, but I am satisfied that I didn't become a chief.)

(Explanation of why they wore the helmets they wore. The buffalo head meant great endurance. Some animals there had no power and had no right to be on the helmet. The eagle and the horse also had great endurance. These were to represent the people's endurance. The snake meant poison to the people. War itself is terrible,)

The smoke cleared away now and the warriors were in the fourth ascent. You could hear war all over the world. As they appeared, smoke covered up the herb and there was nothing but a skeleton as the smoke cleared away. This war was happening all over the world and the fourth ascent is yet to come. Then when the four riders reached the fourth ascent they turned into black-tailed deer. (Some black-tailed deer are sacred and if you try to kill them you cannot do it.) These deer had wounds on their sides which shone out like lightning. Here they showed me the power of the medicine and how to use it. Then the deer turned around and faced the herb from the east side. The black-horned man was standing there again and he changed himself into a gopher, then into an herb, and next into a skeleton.

(While performing his duties as a medicine man, Black Elk would hear women singing all over the room.)

The black spirit says: "Behold your herb; with it everything you face will be like it and the world will tremble." (meaning that whenever I have the herb I will be able to destroy). (Dispute of four ascents means war in the four quarters.) "There shall be a dispute of the winds, and then you shall depend upon the herb."

During this whole time I did not notice how I was dressed. But now I noticed that I was painted red and all my joints were black. There was a white stripe between the joints all over my body. And wherever I would breathe, I would be breathing lightning. My bay horse had lightning stripes on it. The horse's name was like clouds.

Linda L. Stampoulos

Black Elk returns to the six grandfathers

They took me back to where the grandfathers were now. "Behold, you shall go back to where your grandfathers are." Then I saw the rainbow flaming and I saw the six grandfathers sitting there. (I had seemed to be traveling with them, but I found I was traveling toward them instead.) Then I saw the first two men (turned into geese) that I had seen in the beginning of the vision. They were flying in four formations (circles)—one over the east, one over the west, one over the north, one over the south. The nation of geese sang this:

In four circles they are flying.
In a sacred manner.
May you behold them.

As they went around, the geese called thus: "B-p-p-p, b-p-p-p!" On earth Black Elk is to make the goose sound and he will get the goose power. The western spirit said: "Behold them, for they shall have a sacred voice for you." Here I was presented with the power of the goose voice,

They were taking me back now. Now I could see the house of the first grandfather. It was walled and roofed with cloud and above was lightning and underneath were the fowls of the air. Under the fowls are the beasts of the earth and men. The people on earth were rejoicing and the birds and animals and lightning and thunder were like laughter. They were saying: "Eagle Wing Stretches is coming home." Just before I entered the house, the black spirit said: "Behold your grandfathers; a great council they are having." The door was facing the side where the sun shines continually.

As I entered the door the grandfathers cheered for me. I could hear many voices cheering. They were praising me. Some of them said: "He has triumphed!" As I entered, all the grandfathers were sitting with their arms and palms out and said: "He has triumphed!" I could see nothing but millions of faces behind the grandfathers. The west spirit said (pointing to all the people trying to see me): "Behold your nation!"

(All the six men had wooden cups of water in front of them.) I took the cup of water from the west spirit and I could see a buffalo in the water. He presented it to me saying: "Behold the cup; in this cup your nation and you shall feed from it." (Meaning that this cup will be used for me and my nation—that they will all be relatives to each other, and the water is the power to give them strength and to purify them. This water will make the people happy.)

Again I looked toward the people and took good notice this time. I saw there were some people in there of different tribes that I was to get along with on earth. I wasn't quite sure yet whether I saw a white man or not. (What I saw there actually happened, for now I have friends of all different tribes, even of the whites. There will probably never be a time again when the Indians will fight each other; but the whites will fight each other and the Indians may have to fight in with the whites.) The people were happy, as I could see, after I took the cup.

The second (northern) grandfather spoke: "Grandson, all around the universe you have seen the powers and for what you have done your people rejoiced. You have given the men of earth the power they have given you, and with courage they are facing the wind" (meaning the wind of life). Hundreds shall be sacred; hundreds shall be flames." He came forward and put butterfly cocoons onto my arms—a red one on the right wrist and a brown one on the left wrist. (Brown is sacred and red is lightning power. "All over the universe, all your grandfathers, the two-leggeds and on-earth walking, the day-fliers, they have had a council and appointed you and have given you their power. Now you shall go forth to the place from whence you came. Your people are in great difficulty. Behold them!"

As they (the grandfathers) said that I turned around and I could see that it was my own people. Everyone was happy and all the horses were happy except one who was sick. I took good notice and it was myself and I had been sick twelve days. This was probably the twelfth day when I was just going back to my body. I was shown the village and the second grandfather presented me with a cup of water, saying: "Behold this cup." In this cup I saw a man painted blue and he had a bow and arrow and he was in distress. He wanted to get out of the water and get away, but I was told to drink it down. They said: "Make haste and drink your cup of water." I took it and drank the man too. This blue spirit was a fish and I had drunk it down. From this I received strange power and whenever I was conjuring (wapia) I could actually make this blue man come out and swim in the cup of water I used. (The fish represents the power of the water.)

The black spirit says: "Stand over to the third grandfather." (As each grandfather finished talking he would melt into the earth and come up again. Each time a grandfather spoke I was nearer to the earth.)

The third grandfather speaks: "Behold, there are two days relative-like they have given you." Pointing the cup of water to me he said: "Behold this; like unto this you shall live." There was a star in the third cup of water. He said again: "On earth the beings will be glad to see you. So take courage. Now you shall go back to your mother earth." Through this morning star in the cup of water I was to get all my wisdom to know everything.

The black spirit said to me again: "Stand over to the fourth grandfather." The fourth grandfather said (as he presented me with the cup I noticed the red road across the cup): "The road of the generations you shall walk. The ascents of your days shall be sacred. Take courage, your grandfathers shall watch over you in all the four quarters of the earth.

The fourth grandfather sang this song:

There is somebody lying on earth in a sacred manner.
I made him walk. (five times)
There is somebody, on earth he lies.
In a sacred manner I have caused him to walk.

(Black Elk uses this song in treating the sick.)

The black spirit says to me: "Stand over by the fifth grandfather." Then I noticed a cup which represented the Great Spirit. In this cup was a spotted eagle outstretched. "Your grandfathers, whatever they have decided upon, you have finished. Take this." The eagle began to make beautiful sounds and I noticed his eyes were sparkling and he (the eagle) was dancing. "Every day this eagle shall be over you. He has eyes that will see everything (living eyes), and through them you shall also see. To your nation in a sacred manner you shall go."

The black spirit again asked me to stand over to the sixth grandfather. The sixth grandfather showed me a cup full of water and in it there were small human beings. He said: "Behold them, with great difficulty they shall walk and you shall go among them. You shall make six centers of the nation's hoop." (Referring to the six cups of water, meaning that the six centers of the nation's hoop were the different bands or tribes: the Oglala, Hunkpapa, Sicangu, Minnicoujou, Itazipco, and the Shihela , (also included are the Oohenumpa, and the Siha Sapa.)

"Behold them, this is your nation and you shall go back to them. There are six centers of your nation and there you shall go. Now in a scared manner you shall walk. Your grandfathers shall make four goals" (four quarters).

Now the cloud house began to sway back and forth and everyone was moving around in it. The rainbow over the house was moving up and down. "Behold, the rainbow of your grandfathers shall be set where the sun shines continually." Then I could hear all living voices outside the rainbow tipi calling to me as I came out of the tipi: "Eagle Wing Stretches is coming out, so behold him!" Now I noticed the sixth grandfather was myself, who represented the spirit of mankind.

"Your grandfathers have given you a good twelve days of happiness, and you shall have twelve sacred days. A day is appearing—behold its face as you come forth. It is so (hecetu yelo). Your grandfathers shall go forth. You shall lead them. The living creatures of the earth's generations walk together as relatives."

When they showed me the star it was daybreak and then the sun came up and after it appeared they told me to go forth and I stood outside the rainbow tipi and this was the happiest moment of the vision. I looked to the four quarters of the earth and I saw all the riders. There were colors and lightning in the west and I saw black horses. In the north there were all kinds of birds flying and all different colors of horses. The same was true of the east. All sorts of horses started to mill around and in the south the buckskins were milling around. On earth the animals all rejoiced in happiness.

When I came out of the rainbow tipi the sixth grandfather was gone and I stood there in his place. The western grandfather led me out and the horses all neighed as I came out. As each grandfather came out of the rainbow tipi he was cheered for, they all took their places—north, south and east. As the eastern man came out he took the rainbow with him and set it on the east side. The last grandfather was on earth and I did not know it and when I started to come back I was suddenly left alone. I heard a voice saying: "Look back and behold it." I looked back and the cloud house was gone. There was nothing there but a big mountain with a big gap in it. (Black Elk knows where this mountain is—Pike's Peak.)

The Spotted Eagle guides Black Elk home

I could see nothing but dust flying on the four quarters of the earth. I looked up and could see right above me a spotted eagle hovering over me and this was evidently who told me to look back. I started back to the camp with the eagle guarding me. No one was with me then but the eagle, but I knew that I was coming back to the center of the nation's hoop by myself. I could see the people following me. Soon I saw my own tipi at home and I walked fast to get there. As I entered the tipi I saw a boy lying there dying and I stood there awhile and finally found out that it was myself.

The next thing I heard was somebody saying: "The boy is feeling better now, you had better give him some water." I looked up and saw it was my mother and father stooping over me. They were giving me some medicine but it was not that that cured me—it was my vision that cured me. The first thought that came to me was that I had been traveling and my father and mother didn't seem to know that I had been gone and they didn't look glad. I felt very sad over this.

Linda L. Stampoulos

"The Daybreak Star gives the promise of more light to come." Black Elk reminds us that the promise of the future is with our young people, and those not yet born. Their light will shine on the good Red Road and help us find the way back inside the sacred hoop. Photo is provided by the Denver Public Library, Western History Collection, (Circa 1890) Call Number X31545.

SUGGESTED READING

Bailey, Paul. *Ghost Dance Messiah*. Tucson: Westernlore Press, 1986.

Brown, Joseph Epes, ed. *The Sacred Pipe: Black Elk's Account of the Seven Rites of the Oglala Sioux*. Norman: University of Oklahoma Press, 1953.

Campbell, Joseph. *The Hero with a Thousand Faces*. Princeton: Princeton University Press, 1949.

Campbell, Joseph. *The Masks of God: Primitive Mythology*. New York: Viking Penguin, Inc., 1959.

Campbell, Joseph. *The Masks of God: Occidental Mythology*. New York: Viking Penguin, Inc. 1964.

Campbell, Joseph. *Myths To Live By*. New York: Viking Penguin, Inc., 1972.

Clowser, Don C. *Dakota Indian Treaties. From Nomad to Reservation*. Don C. Clowser, Deadwood, 1974.

DeMallie, Raymond J. ed. *The Sixth Grandfather: Black Elk's Teachings Given to John G. Neihardt*. Lincoln: University of Nebraska Press, 1984.

Halifax, Joan. *Shaman, The Wounded Healer*. New York: Thames and Hudson Inc. 1982.

Jung, Carl Gustav. *The Archetypes and the Collective Unconscious*. from the Collected Works of C.G. Jung, Volume 9, Part I. Princeton:: Princeton University Press, 1969.

Means, Russell. with Marvin J. Wolf. *Where White Men Fear to Tread, The Autobiography of Russell Means*. New York: St. Martin's Griffin, 1995.

Mooney, James. *The Ghost-Dance Religion and the Sioux Outbreak of 1890.* Smithsonian Institution, Bureau of American Ethnology, Annual Report 14, Pt. 2, 1896.

Neihardt, John G. *Black Elk Speaks: Being the Life Story of a Holy Man of the Oglala Sioux.* New York: William Morrow & Co., 1932.

Neihardt, John G. *When the Tree Flowered: The story of Eagle Voice, a Sioux Indian.* Lincoln: University of Nebraska Press, (New Edition), 1991.

Neihardt, Hilda. *Black Elk and Flaming Rainbow: Personal Memories of the Lakota Holy Man and John Neihardt.* Lincoln: University of Nebraska Press, 1995.

Shields, Kenneth. *Fort Peck Indian Reservation, Montana.* Charleston, S.C.: Arcadia Publishing, 1998.

Shields, Kenneth. *The Little Bighorn, Tiospaye.* Chicago: Arcadia Publishing, 1998.

Sprague, Donovin Arleigh. *Cheyenne River Sioux.* Chicago: Arcadia Publishing, 2003.

Sprague, Donovin Arleigh. *Pine Ridge Reservation.* Chicago: Arcadia Publishing, 2004.

Sprague, Donovin Arleigh. *Standing Rock Sioux.* Chicago: Arcadia Publishing, 2004.

Stampoulos, Linda L. *Visiting the Grand Canyon: Views of Early Tourism.* Chicago: Arcadia Publishing, 2004. Listed as one of Southwest Books of the Year – Best Reading 2004.

Stampoulos, Linda L., and Zanger, Scott L. *Two on a Bridge.* Publication date: Winter 2006.

Walker, James R. *Lakota Belief and Ritual.* Edited by Raymond J. DeMallie and Elaine A. Jahner. Lincoln: University of Nebraska Press, 1980.

Walker, James R. *Lakota Society.* Edited by Raymond J. DeMallie. Lincoln: University of Nebraska Press, 1982.

www.ingramcontent.com/pod-product-compliance
Lightning Source LLC
Chambersburg PA
CBHW041615220426
43671CB00001B/2